IN THE GARDEN *of* HEARTS

IN THE GARDEN
of HEARTS

MEDITATIONS, CONSOLATIONS, *and* BLESSINGS *for* TEACHERS

PETE REILLY

IRIMI HORIZONS

ISBN 978-0-9861354-1-5

Irimi Horizons Publishing

Tomkins Cove, NY 10986

www.petereilly.org

www.preilly.wordpress.org

Cover and book design by Tom McKeveny

DEDICATED TO JOHN O'DONOHUE

priest, poet, philosopher, and Irishman.

Bless the space between us.

Table of Contents

Part 2: THE CHALLENGE

Part 3: THE HEART

Part 4: THE HARVEST

PREFACE

The material in this book is not filled with new ideas and information but is simply a reminder of the true nature of our purpose as educators. The meditations and blessings within it are markers that point us in the direction of things which we already know but which are easily forgotten amidst the day to day stresses and routines of teaching.

Each meditation and blessing is meant to provide you with space...space to step back and look at teaching, and your life, from a different perspective, a wider lens that may open the doors to new ways of thinking about your 'self', your classroom, and your students.

In the Garden of Hearts is not meant to be read cover to cover in a linear fashion, but rather to be a resource to turn to when you're in need of support, perspective, or inspiration. It's a book that should be at hand when drinking your morning coffee or kept on your nightstand for a few minutes of reading before bed.

Throughout the book I define teaching in its broadest sense and include in that definition therapists, leadership coaches, mentors, counselors, and all those that seek to guide others to a better life.

In addition to more than sixty original pieces, I've included works from teaching masters like Fr. Dennis Moormon, a Catholic priest who works with victims of physical and emotional trauma. There is a thoughtful exploration of the gifts that silence offers written by Jeanne Denney, a therapist, teacher, hospice worker, and death (and life) educator. I also include a poem by Chase Miele, a candidate for Teacher of the Year in Michigan, as well as an autobiographical parable written by Dr. Patrick B. Awosogba, Sr., the founding principal of Mott Hall Science and Technology Academy, an amazingly successful public school in NYC's South Bronx.

In the Garden of Hearts includes a mix of Zen Koans, Celtic and Native American wisdom, interpretations of stories that I've collected over the years, as well as meditative pieces and excerpts from the Tao Te Ching, Rumi, Kahil Gibran, and Rainer Maria Rilke.

Throughout the book I use the metaphor of teachers as 'gardeners' and classrooms as 'gardens'. I believe that we're each truly blessed to have been called to serve the world as teachers. May you find peace and joy in whatever "Garden of Hearts" you're privileged to tend.

INTRODUCTION

On the last day of a recent trip to Ireland I was guided by Courtney Davis, a talented local artist and painter, to a sacred well that flowed from the side of the Hill of Tara. Lying on my stomach I inched my upper body into the stone opening leaving the wide sky smiling above me and the green grasses whispering in the early evening's dying light. The world outside now gone, I lay prone in the dim interior which was as silent and majestic in its simplicity as the great cathedrals of Europe in all their grandeur.

It seemed the well was dry and I was disappointed. But I reached down into the dark with my hand and suddenly there came the sweet caress of water so clear that neither my eyes nor my mind had initially discerned its presence. Sometimes thresholds are like that, invisible before our eyes and hidden from our minds. It takes reaching our trusting hands into what seems like nothingness to discover them.

The water was a cool and silent gift from the secret world that flowed under the hill of the kings of Tara. It was an embrace from Maeve, the Earth Goddess herself who allowed me to rest my head in the wellspring of her bosom for a brief moment. My own heart seemed renewed by the ancient cleansing water. I found myself whispering a silent blessing,

"May I cultivate and use my gifts to nurture the hearts of teachers."

I didn't drink the water but my thirst was quenched and as unlikely as it may seem, this book was born.

But where did this blessing come from? To whom was it addressed? What was it about the Well of Tara that motivated me to whisper it? And what was it that my blessing was asking to bring forth? For the sake of what?

These questions linger with me even as I write this today. There are many layers to the answers and not all lead to tidy explanations. In fact, the most meaningful questions often lead to more questions. The great poet Rainer Maria Rilke wrote,

> "Be patient toward all that is unsolved in your heart and try to love the questions themselves, like locked rooms and like books that are now written in a very foreign tongue. Do not now seek the answers, which cannot be given you because you would not be able to live them. And the point is, to live everything. Live the questions now. Perhaps you will then gradually, without noticing it, live along some distant day into the answer."

And so I live in the questions that began long before I crawled into the well gouged from the side of the Hill of Tara. While the questions persist so does my belief that each of us longs to have our lives mean something and that great teachers must willingly give themselves over to the questions this yearning brings forth.

Blessings

I use the format of blessings throughout this book. These are secular blessings though they may lead us to the parts of ourselves that open onto the vast horizons of the spirit...the heart. A blessing is a calling forth of kindness from some inner well of the infinite. It's a testament to faith.

These blessings are meant to remind ourselves that we're creatures of the heart and that as teachers we work "In the Garden of Hearts". They call us away from the busy-ness of the professional world to the quiet universe of the sacred well that each of us has within us. It's within this boundless interior space that grace allows us to break free of deadening routines and awakens us to the incredible world in which we live. It's in this space that we transform anger into compassion, doubt into action, and hate into love. It's a place where we can turn toward our fears knowing that they call us to new thresholds, thresholds that we are finally ready to cross, our hearts having been working in silence these many years to prepare us for the journey.

The blessings in this book ask us to slow down, to breathe, to shift our attention from life's shiny objects that garner so much of our energy and attention, in order to walk the quiet paths of the heart. They beckon to us to linger in a secret garden filled with scents and sounds that are so subtle that they're invisible to us in our daily rush. The moment we stop our hurrying and sit in silence, (or perhaps reach into the darkness of a sacred well), an entirely different world comes into focus.

In their own way blessings can overwhelm us with their simplicity for they bear witness to the world of our hearts where there are no fears or anxieties, no complicated rationalizations, and no withholding. It's a landscape of unconditional acceptance, call it love, of ourselves and of all things around us. This simple inner wisdom oftentimes conflicts with our tactical and strategic mind with its penchant for control and need for guarantees of safety. A blessing can call us to surrender to the unknown while our minds are shouting for us to hold on to the familiar, or it can call us to persevere when we feel like giving up. It can invite us to consider compassion in the midst of self-righteousness, or ask us to make a courageous choice to act when doing nothing would be much easier.

Blessings call us to the frontiers of our experience. They ask us to perfect and share our gifts and to recognize and express our gratitude for the gifts of others. In the bosom of the blessing is the willingness to carry the burdens of others and the hope that others will be willing to carry ours, that is if we can learn to allow ourselves to be carried. Yes, a blessing is something to give and in the giving to receive.

My hope is that this book will support, console, and inspire the many thousands of educators who selflessly dedicate their lives to "heart-fully" tending their classroom gardens and the children within them. It's within these gardens that new generations of children awaken to the wonder of words, the majesty of math, and the beauty of the arts and science. But most important of all, it's the place where so many discover their unique gifts, their purpose, and where they begin to fully participate in the ongoing conversation that is life itself.

MORE ABOUT BLESSINGS

For those of us who work in the "Garden of Hearts" the blessings in this book are an invitation to seek the dimly lit places in our own hearts. As we explore this rich interior landscape we soon recognize it as a place that brings us face to face with our elemental fears. How much of our true selves can we reveal to others? Should we risk rejection? Do we really belong? Are we loved? These fears are sometimes amplified by the limiting beliefs about ourselves that we've accumulated over the years. We may believe that deep down we're "less than", or that we're untalented, weak, cowardly, unattractive, or lazy. The list of negative beliefs that we, as human beings, carry with us could fill this page and many others.

But blessings speak past our fears and limiting beliefs to the goodness and wisdom that resides in our hearts. They call us to step out of the shadows to acknowledge the miracle of being alive. What greater miracle can we imagine than being a part of this amazing world? It's a strange but common aspect of the human condition that even something as unique, precious, and miraculous as life itself can become familiar and mundane. All too often we hear the words, "I'm bored." Blessings help open us, for an instant, to the incredible abundance of our natural inheritance.

But to be effective a blessing must also be connected to our basic human concerns and for the purposes of this book to our work as teachers. To be in service to others (our students) we must take exquisite care of ourselves, body, mind, and spirit. So blessings summon us to our own wisdom and capacity for self-healing.

Abandoning our need to control, manipulate, and antici-pate the events that impact our lives is difficult, even though we know deep in our hearts that pursuing them is a "fool's errand". Surrendering to the summons of our inner wisdom isn't giving up, it's opening up.

Blessings can transform a familiar morning routine into a rite of celebration and gratitude. Each morning when we awaken from the mysterious universe of dreams we open our eyes to a world filled with new possibilities. Each precious day provides us with an opportunity to take a new path, to open a new door, to ask a new question. The Russian poet Anatoly Ivaneshki writes in his poem "The Non-Conformist",

> Men and women love the dawn for its freshness,
> for its promise of new beginnings,
> in the morning therefore,
> I am not frightened that I have chosen to live
> a life unlike that of other young men.

His words, like the blessings in this book, are a reminder of our longing to come home to ourselves, to choose to live the one life we have on our own terms, for it's all too easy to live a life that isn't really ours, a life that we've shaped to be acceptable to others, abandoning our innermost yearnings for the promise of safety, membership in the group, the larger culture, and society. A blessing is an invitation to awaken to ourselves and to claim the power we have to build a life that fully expresses the gift we are, and manifests the gifts we have.

As teachers, we must experience this awakening ourselves before we can authentically enter the "Garden of Hearts" and begin our work. Plato says in "The Symposium" that one of the greatest privileges of a human life is to become midwife to the birth of the soul in another. What a gift it is to work with children, to be in the position to be such a midwife. We work in a very special garden but it's quite easy for us to take the privilege for granted and go about our business never thinking of our hearts, or theirs.

Blessings, meditations, and consolations are meant to offer solace, perspective, and inspiration for we educators who are under pressure to eliminate a special project that students love because it takes time and isn't fully correlated to the standards, or for those of us who are considering eliminating a great novel, a class discussion, debate, scientific experiment, class trip or some other memorable experience to make room for more practice on skills that will show up on state and national tests. Blessings remind us of our larger purpose and call us to be true to the wisdom of our own hearts.

I have faith in our teaching corp. I see many, many new teachers entering the profession with big ideas and armed with a deep commitment to helping others in service to a purpose larger than themselves. My hope is that this book will support, console, and inspire them, as well the many thousands of 'seasoned' educators who selflessly dedicate their lives to "heart-fully" tending their classroom gardens and the children within them.

May these blessing serve as a refuge for those who dare to take a "road less traveled", and those who are committed to keeping teaching an endeavor of the heart.

A Blessing for Your Classroom

Your classroom is your home.
May no student ever leave it
without receiving a blessing or gift,
no matter how small.

May it be a place where you can be yourself,
find yourself, cultivate yourself,
for there is no better crucible
to test your beliefs and values
than this classroom.

May students look forward to entering this space.
May they flock to you and embrace you with questions.
May their laughter spill through the door
and echo in the empty hallways

May this room be an invitation to possibility,
and frontiers to be explored.
May what goes on here each day
mean something, change something,
contribute to a purpose larger than yourself.

May you truly appreciate this classroom
as a microcosm of the world.
May it be a safe place.
A place of peace.

A place of learning for your students,
and for you.

This is your garden,
may the soil be rich.

THE JOURNEY

"Not all those who wander are lost."

J.R.R. TOLKIEN

Joseph Campbell, the noted philosopher once said, "The cave you fear to enter holds the treasure you seek." The teacher's journey is the hero's journey, which, if you're reading this, just so happens to be the journey you're on. It's a journey that each of us travels from the moment of our birth, for life is not linear and death is not a far off thing penciled in on our calendar for a much later date. Death lives as a possibility in the midst of every breath we take. Awakening to this knowledge rouses us from our comfortable daydreams, and calls us to make the most of our lives…to take the first steps on the unfamiliar path that the hero must travel.

The true nature of our quest is not to change the world, (though it may do so) but to change ourselves. Our journey can begin at any time. It's always there waiting for us to arrive for it's a journey that is just right for us and no one else. Often we arrive unexpectedly at its threshold as did the traveler in Dante's *Inferno*,

> At the mid-point of the path through life, I found
> Myself lost in a wood so dark, the way
> Ahead was blotted out…

> …And I can't say even now how I had come
> To be there, stunned and following my nose
> Away from the straight path.

While the traveler in this verse finds himself lost at the "mid-point" of his life, not sure how he arrived in the "dark wood" "Away from the straight path", we might encounter our own 'dark night of the soul' long before we reach midlife. As fearful and upsetting as that can be, it may be a "blessing in disguise" because with the way ahead "blotted out" we're forced to step into the unknown in order to find our way forward. It's a place, if given a choice, many of us would choose to avoid. In truth, many of us do. Often it takes a sudden heart attack, a divorce, the loss of a job, or some other life trauma to awaken us to the fact that we're lost.

Whether we find ourselves stunned to be lost in the woods not knowing the way forward or whether we decide, courageously, that our lives are only a shadow of our true selves and decide that we will no longer be actors in a play that someone else has written, choreographed and directed; when we commit ourselves to becoming the authors of our own lives, our hero's odyssey, our journey to teaching mastery has begun.

For most of us this is a spiritual pilgrimage, for the sacred place we seek to find and the wisdom we need to bring us there, is largely within us. Whether our hero's task is to slay a metaphorical dragon that holds us hostage in its greedy yearning for safety and security (even if it means living an empty life sitting alone in a dark cave atop a mountain of gold), or whether it means facing some long held and most fearful of fears, the journey is largely within.

It's within the unfamiliar "wood so dark", or as Campbell calls it, the "cave that you fear," that we are brought to the edge of our capacities. While all our successes and everything we've learned has led us to this place, our past experiences are not enough to bring us where we need to go. In the midst of the unknown, at a threshold leading to some new life, we feel completely and totally disarmed. Our strategic minds can't think our way back to the safety and successes of the past, or find a convenient way for us to escape our moment of truth.

Stripped of our usual defenses and seemingly alone we suddenly find ourselves relying on an organic wisdom that surfaces at just the right instant…when we need it the most and are most ready to accept it. It's within the wildness of this unpredictable and terrifying moment that we are called to trust ourselves and surrender to the wisdom of our own heart. It's a kind of death of the old self to make way for the new.

To be sure there is no way to make this journey easily. I suppose that's the point. We live in a crucible of our own making. The hero's journey, the teacher's journey, is meant to reveal the essence of our character, often hidden deep within us. The unknown can be the best friend a soul can have because when we fully engage it, without control or guarantees of safe passage, we find ourselves fully alive.

What courage it takes to let go! What faith in ourselves and in the unfolding of life we must have! For there are no guarantees of happy endings, at least not in the short run, for we know there will surely be discomfort and suffering as we feel our way forward on this new path.

Of course we don't have to make this pilgrimage alone. As John O'Donohue says, "A burden shared is a burden halved." There are people around us who have traveled this way before, although on their own path in their own way, but they can support us, guide us, provide us with a peaceful place to rest when rest is needed. However, the last courageous step on the hero's journey, like death itself, must be taken by us, and us alone.

Once this step is taken we're ready to return to the old world where we began our adventure…but we aren't the same. Our hero's journey, our "dark night of the soul", has pushed us to, and through, our limits and over a new threshold. We're transformed. We emerge a different person. This is especially relevant for those of us that choose to teach because having taken the hero's journey we're better equipped to work "In the Garden of Hearts" and better able to awaken our students to their own heroic journeys which are always ready and waiting for them.

Teaching is a profession rooted in the heart and to master it we're called to the hero's journey, the challenging path of self-discovery.

Your Calling

Stirs within you silently like a powerful tide
swelling in the silver light of a full moon.

It speaks to a different part of you,
not the mind with its strategies
calculating the odds of security, money and success,
but in the unfamiliar language of yearning.

This innocent but fearful longing
brings you to the edge of a new river
where you stand, awed by its roiling currents,
a strangely familiar beckoning
calling you towards it's cleansing waters.

You wonder from where the waters come
and where they flow, and why,
while your mind shouts for you to turn back
to the well worn concrete highway
where cars rush frantically and well lit signs
    light the way.

Your confusion is a cairn marking your journey's progress,
there is no need to turn back,
you are exactly where you need to be.

Have faith that your calling is not a problem
    to be solved
but a problem sent to solve you,
to help you lose yourself,
and in this losing to find something eternal,
    meaningful, and real,
for you are called to a journey not a job,
a life, not simply an occupation.

The stakes are high.
It's easy to follow steps someone else has laid out for you,
and play a role rather than live a life.

How difficult to take the first step on a path
that leads to a destination that can't be seen or
    found on any map.

Your calling is a letting go.

May you have faith in yourself
and the larger forces and currents of life,
in things that can't be seen or controlled
    in the usual way.

May you heed the voice of your own wisdom
and trust in the truth of your own heart.

May you tether yourself to a purpose larger than yourself
and use it to navigate through all the sufferings
    and joys of this life.

And as with all journeys,
may the traveler who finally arrives at her destination
not be the same person who began it.

Starting the Journey

There's no perfect time to begin the journey
you know you must take.
The right time is always now.

Your first courageous step, so difficult,
is taken in the dark, fearfully,
trusting your heart to lead you to a new place.

As you walk this path with no landmarks,
shrouded in chilly morning fog,
you begin to awaken as from a long restless slumber,
a dreamless sleep,
your heart stumbling forward in unfamiliar surroundings.

As you travel,
the savage winds and gentle breezes of self-discovery
    grip you,
and fellow travelers appear to support you.

Be kind to them and to yourself.

Rest when rest is called for.
Sleep on the soft green moss at the edge of the cool pond,
and let your heart be at peace.

May each step on your journey be taken by a slightly
    different you,
but may you never forget who is walking,
where you have come from,
and where you're going.

May your life's journey always lead towards your self,
    never away.

The First Day of School

You scan the faces of your new class
the way a farmer studies his field before planting,
full of hope for a healthy harvest,
understanding the uncertainties of nature,
anticipating days of thankless labor,
but filled with excitement nonetheless,
for it's the seeding, the careful nurturing,
cultivating what each student has within them
that is at the heart of your calling.

You begin the new year not quite sure where
    it will lead,
but present and open in this moment,
full of amazement as the wheels of life turn,
the past disappears,
and the possibilities of new horizons are born.

May you see your students with fresh eyes
and recognize they too look to you
with a longing to be recognized,
to be seen and loved for who they are,
to discover the gifts that wait quietly
in the deep and silent wells of their hearts.

May you fill the blank canvas of the new year
not only with the prose of science and math,

but also with the music and poetry that each
　　has to offer,
as does every subject and every text.

And may you come to understand
that you must find this beauty within yourself
and your own knowing
before helping your students find it
　　for themselves.

May you feel the joy in the voices rising
in a clamor from the playground,
the music echoing from the band room
drifting through the empty halls,
the smell of lunches being prepared,
and the chaotic energy of children
walking, talking, and laughing with their peers,
every word and gesture, loud or soft
a hand feeling for a hold
and a place in the world.

May you be as constant as the seasons
for these young travelers,
and be for them a loving embrace,
a perfect Fall day
bathed in sunlight and warmth,
never to be forgotten.

What It Means to Teach

A young librarian was sent to a remote region of Canada to bring computers to the area's small town libraries. One of the libraries was located on the land of the First People. After the new computers were installed the young man went to each library to train the staff, which in the case of the First People, was a lovely middle aged woman.

The passionate young man spent the entire day training the local librarian on how to use the computer. She was very curious and asked many questions which he was happy to answer. Before he departed the young man asked the native woman whether she understood how to work the computer, to which she replied, "Yes". He asked whether she had any other questions to which she replied, "No". "Great," he said, "I'll be back in a few weeks to see how things are going and I'll answer any questions that might come up while I'm gone." With that he left.

Several weeks later he returned and when he checked the new computer he found that it hadn't been used at all. He didn't ask why she didn't use it but patiently began going over the same material he had taught her on his last visit. He spent the whole day re-teaching his lesson. Once again, before he left, he asked the friendly native woman if she understood what he had taught her, and again she answered, "Yes." The young man felt good about his work and he was proud that he had been so patient with this particularly challenging student. After all, some people might have been frustrated with having to repeat the same lesson a second time.

On his next trip to the little library the young man was surprised to find that the computer had still not been used. He was confused. When he asked the librarian, "Why?", she looked embarrassed and shrugged her shoulders. For a third time he repeated his lesson, but this time his voice betrayed his frustration. He was thinking, "What's wrong with this woman? I don't think she'll ever get this!" He was angry at her.

When the teacher was done for the day he didn't ask the woman whether she understood what he had taught her. He left in anger and went immediately to the office of the tribal leader and complained to him, "Every time I train her she says she understands, but when I come back, it's clear she doesn't. I've gone over the same material exactly the same way three times now and I don't think she'll ever get it. There's something wrong with her! Maybe we should try to get someone else for the job."

The tribal leader got up from behind his desk and put his arm around the young man's shoulders and began speaking as if sharing a secret, "You don't understand do you? She's a very good person and she's trying to be very polite and not hurt your feelings. You see, in our culture if she's not learning it's doesn't reflect on her. It reflects on you. After all, you're the teacher."

There was a long silence. The young man looked into the smiling eyes of the tribal elder and saw his own reflection. Suddenly he realized who it was that had failed the lesson. It was at this very moment that he became a teacher.

For Morning Routines – Home

Each morning brings the possibility of a fresh start to our lives.
Sometimes we abandon our dreams too quickly and rush too readily
into the rhythms of the day. What if we lingered in the space
between sleep and awakening for a few extra moments, waking
deliberately, allowing ourselves to participate in the calm silence
that flows through the ongoing conversation that is our life?

On this morning of a new day,
as the dawn's freshness greets you
with its promise of new beginnings,
and you swim in the sweet waters
of peace and contentment,
may your awakening be a rising prayer.

May you say a thousand thank you's
before your feet touch the floor.

Morning after morning you abandon
the comfort of dreams and sleep
at the moment of your awakening,
letting the full force of the current
that is the river of the day,
pull you, drive you, drown you,
before you can catch your breath,
letting your mind be swept away
in the rapid currents of urgency.

Today, remember the lilies of the field
and trust that all you need to do can be done.
Put away worry and endless planning.
Allow yourself to relax into the first breath of morning,
and open yourself slowly to the new day.

Though your days are full
and you find yourself rushing
from task to task, thought to thought,
thinking, always thinking, of what needs to get done,
has to get done, must get done;
on this day may you never stray
too far from the ground of your body and
    the clay of your heart.

May your morning mind be peaceful and
    wander where it will,
dreaming, stretching,
feeling the stirrings of new life
in the simple rituals and ablutions of awakening.

Let your first breath this morning,
be a question answered with silence.

For Morning Routines - Classroom

Schools and classrooms are overflowing with frenetic energy. We're called to be 'on' from the earliest moments of the day. Rarely do we experience the sacredness of solitude. Deliberately carving out a few minutes to bring ourself present to the things we care about can effect the entire day.

Listen in silence to the rushing energy
of life stirring within the building,
comings and goings, voices, laughter,
the routine of early morning a familiar comfort.

Anything is possible this day.
You can choose to live it like no other.

Before the first student breaks the quiet solitude,
let your breath bring you present to this moment,
open you to the day's possibilities,
and keep you connected to the things you care about.

May your heart be a satin butterfly kissed by sunshine,
carried on its long migration by a favorable wind,
and sustained by the brilliant flowers
that fill your classroom.

May each child be free to embark on their own journey
to lands you may never see.

This classroom is no ordinary workplace.
What goes on here this day, though planned
        carefully on paper,
carries the promise of something wild and grand,
a courageous encounter with truth,
a glowing ember capable of igniting
some terrifying and wondrous passion
in your students and your self.

May your ears hear your students' voices,
their utterances and their silences,
as well as the patient voice of your own knowing
which calls you this morning to awaken,
for you are both teacher
and student.

Raising a Hand

Bless the child who raises her hand to attempt an answer,
share a thought, tell a story,
or ask a question,
for it is an act of courageous connection.

She is stepping forward to be seen,
to be heard,
feeling worthy of attention,
trusting you to hold the space for the tender unfolding
of her delicate new wings,
placing her 'self' in your carefully cupped hands.

May you keep her safe.

Pause

Bless the pause
which like the gloaming between darkness
   and breaking dawn,
the brief instant between in-breath and out breath,
the last sounds of night mixing with those
   of the awakening day,
reveals in this unformed moment,
the true faces of our students
sparkling like diamond dew,
reflecting the radiance of possibility.

Bless the pause that breaks the momentum of anger
that grips us and threatens to explode in a
   torrent of thunder,
the pause that allows us to reclaim ourselves
from the wreckage of our own selfish habits
and long held patterns of behavior.

May this infinitesimal crack
separating past and future
be a refuge of peace
a place of rebirth
and a garden of renewal.

For Patience

The smaller and more crowded the world gets, the more difficult the work of maintaining our patience both in and out of the classroom. Instant gratification is the order of the day. Fast food, fast cars, and a jam packed curriculum, meet head on with indigestion, slower traffic, and more students requiring individual attention. As our work becomes more complicated and complex our patience begins to fray. No matter how hard we try, it seems like we're getting nowhere.

Your classroom, like the world,
runs in high gear,
and time is precious.

But learning and understanding increase when
    we slow down
and allow our extended attention to reveal hidden nuances
not available in a glance or scan.

Patience keeps us from succumbing to doubt
for the storm will pass and the spring will come,

Patience allows us to maintain our steady effort.

It takes patience to practice,
patience to fail,
and patience to learn from that failure.

Patience is choosing not to respond without thinking,
but pausing to allow other possibilities to arise.

Patience is much more than repeating the same
    lesson over and over,
but varying our approaches.

When you feel the boundaries of your patience
begin to crumble in frustration,
remember your own fear of being wrong
and looking foolish in front of others.

Maintain your belief in your students
even when they've given up on themselves.

May you remember that true learning comes to us
    when we're ready.

When we are called to it,
our learning is perfect.

May we be infinitely patient with ourselves,
and because we are human beings,
forgive ourselves when we aren't.

Call of the Wild

I was born and blessed, as are each of us, with a natural
curiosity. There was a great wildness in it. As a child I'd see
a shaft of sunlight illuminating a world of dust and delicate
objects floating in the air and I'd stop whatever I was doing
and begin to explore its tiny universe. It was magical. I was
called to learn. Curiosity was my birthright. It was in my
DNA. It's in yours.

My natural curiosity was like a wild animal and it hunted
where it needed in order to satisfy its deep hunger. As a child
I awakened each day with an insatiable appetite to explore,
to discover, to learn. In my early years I was a voracious "wolf
of learning". I believe deep in our DNA there's a relation-
ship between curiosity, learning and survival. We might call it
"the burning relevance of an empty stomach" because in past
millennia our ancestors needed to be voracious learners in
order to survive.

Over the centuries, learning has become institutionalized.
Vast school systems and local and national curricula are now
the norm. And as these institutions have grown they've pushed
aside much of the wildness of our natural curiosity. Looking
back I realize that as I worked my way through the educational
system I became more tame and more timid. I can see now
that in many ways I was being domesticated. I was no longer a
"wolf of learning".

How did this happen? Perhaps it was that I had no
control over my education and whatever natural curiosity I had

was replaced by a structured and scripted curriculum. I was rewarded for following directions and doing what I was told and reprimanded if I let my curiosity wander too far from the prescribed lesson. I was chewing on someone else's agenda and not mine so I simply worked in "compliance mode", putting forth minimum effort. Fear of retribution and bad grades become my prime motivators not the excitement of discovery and learning.

Thus I became a ward of a system that trained me to expect to learn without going on the hunt. Like a domesticated pet I was offered bland processed learning, laid out in prescribed amounts, at certain times of the day. A pre-set curriculum guide that had little to do with me, my interests, my needs, or my gifts, decided what I was fed, how much, and when. I rarely experienced learning by my own wits, my natural curiosity, or even the magic of serendipity. I was no longer the wolf who'd gorge on learning and fight over the scraps until my belly was full.

I'd become so domesticated that I would've rebelled if asked to use the natural gifts for learning with which I was born. It would have been like releasing a pet house dog into the wilderness...the odds of survival would've been small, and within hours I'd have been back at the front door begging to have my master serve dinner to me in a dish.

Now, as an adult, I'm finally rediscovering my own power, wildness, curiosity. My love of learning has been rekindled.

For the sake of our students,

may each of us find our own ways to foster the wildness and thrill of learning in our students...

...and rediscover the "call of the wild".

Silence

Schools are filled with the sounds
of human beings communicating,
teachers explaining and questioning,
children finding the power of their own voices

There is little quiet, little reflection.
Words become cheap,
and ideas are lost in mountains of talk.

May we honor the clarity of silence.
The silence of the fearful.
The silence of the bullied.
The silence of a teacher watching her student
    squander his gifts.
The silence after a great question,
and the silence of students calculating the risk of
    offering an answer.
There is the silence of a teacher who has no
    words to explain
the sacrifices she makes for her students,
and the silence of students who would not understand
    if she did.

There are the silences of those
with secret burdens, fearful and heavy,
and the silence of adolescent doubt.

"Do I belong?" "Am I different?" "Am I loved?"
There is the silence of a great hatred and a great love,
and the generous silence of reflection.

In silence the voice we need to hear speaks loudest.

Hear the Wind

The Eagle wasn't always the Eagle.

The Eagle, before he became the Eagle, was Yucatangee, the Talker.

Yucatangee talked and talked. It talked so much it heard only itself.

Not the river, not the wind, not even the Wolf.

The Raven came and said, "The Wolf is hungry. If you stop talking, you'll hear him. The wind, too. And when you hear the wind, you'll fly."

So, he stopped talking, and became its nature, the Eagle.

The Eagle soared, and its flight said all it needed to say.

> —Spoken by the character Marilyn Whirlwind
> on the television show *Northern Exposure*

Finding a New Way

*In each of our personal and professional lives we eventually encounter
a great challenge that brings us to the edge of our competency and
opens the door to new possibilities.*

Our lives follow familiar paths
but the heart knows there are many roads to travel
and when the time is right,
invites us to find a new way forward.

But what way?

Our path brings us to a rocky shore
amid the restless white waves crashing.
The ocean's horizon beckons
and we know that to move forward
we must leave our shoes behind
for they are of no use to us now.

May we trust that we will find a new way of traveling.

May we have the courage to turn toward our longing
and our fear,
and within it to find
the next step on our journey.
and the next,
and the next.

This is the way.

For the Cost of Caring

Our journey asks that we embrace various paradoxes — like
needing a certain toughness in order to keep our classrooms gentle.

Working with students requires a rough sensitivity.

You dig in the garden's dense soil without gloves,
your hands open, sensitive, tender,
feeling the delicate shoots that grow among the stones
and packed earth of your classroom.

Staying open and feeling,
unselfishly nurturing and protecting these new seedlings
growing in rocky soil,
is your calling.

Your open heart suffers when exposed to
  . the hardness of the world.

May the cost of caring,
the scarring and gnarling of your fingers and heart,
never be a price that is too much to pay.

May you keep the classroom gentle and safe
as you feel your way through obstacles,
your calloused hands hardened to protect the soft souls
of those you teach.

Teacher's Prayer
AUTHOR UNKNOWN

Lord, Please help me,
To strengthen their voices,
bodies and minds,
To express their feelings and
control them sometimes,
To explore what's near
and venture afar,
But most important to love
who they are.

New Initiatives

Year after year new leaders appear in our buildings from somewhere far beyond our classrooms. Each leader brings their own strengths and weaknesses and for better or worse their own motives and associated initiatives. A new initiative can be a heavy burden thrust upon us testing our resilience and humility. It can be an exciting experience that opens us to new horizons or a discouraging distraction from the things we value most.

Just when you feel that teaching
has become a frustrating crescendo of voices
talking over each other,
and new mandates like dark clouds
full of thunder and lightning roll over your classroom
threatening your sanity,
you're asked to try something new.

It can be difficult to look past your feelings of
    powerlessness,
for change is sometimes thrust upon you
by those whose memory of the daily work of teaching
    has faded.

Do not confuse the frailties of those leading change
with the change itself.

New initiatives like stones thrown into a still pond
break the peace with a violent splash.
Don't let the disruption frighten you,
anger you, discourage you,
or cause you to close your heart.

May you be present and open to new possibilities.
May you be humble and willing.
May you understand and live the life of "teacher",
a commitment to perpetual learning.

Let your filter be service to your students.
May you be a loyal gatekeeper, true to their best interests.

May you find time for this new thing,
understanding that it asks you to grow.
How you choose to engage it is a reflection of you.

May you welcome this new initiative like a stranger
    from a distant land
walking the streets of a new country,
speaking a strange language,
determined to fit in.

The success of this stranger will make you stronger.

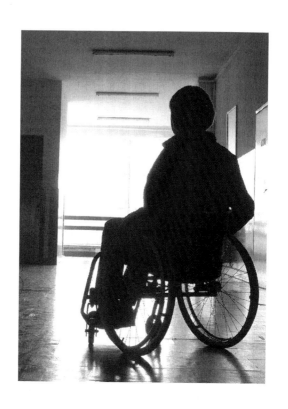

A Student of Silence
Jeanne Denney, MA, P.E.

One could say I am a teacher. Well... I've been teacher. Plenty of times. Primarily, I'm now a teacher of adults and college students. I think of myself as a therapist too. But what taught me most about teaching and the work of the heart was not derived directly from my formal education or even the therapy room. It was from Hospice work.

"Hospice work?" Yes, indeed. Hospice. People old and dying. It was from there I learned that being a great student of the people we think we are "helping" is the best way to do our jobs with heart and avoid burnout. I'd like to tell you a brief story about being a student with some burning questions and what can happen in the silence between two people.

Here is the short of it: After leaving a perfectly respectable career designing bridges at age 41, I found myself training as a healer and volunteering in a Hospice in the most dismal of nursing homes, sitting with people curled in balls and not speaking. I won't give the details. Fortunately, I had little to do but sit and contemplate what was before me. Who was this person? Where were they? What was happening in the silence? How could I reach them? Did they know I was there? Who was I to be here in their presence, in their room? And most importantly, "How could I help?"

Questions abounded. Questions were all I had aside from a scattering of cards on the nightstand and a name. There were no stories. No ego. No identity. No parents. No tests or grades or government targets. Just me and them, both in our vulnerability. One sitting, one lying.

The truth is, I wasn't there as a pure do-gooder. I was an investigator. For reasons I can't give space to, I was there to ask "What can you teach me?" "What do you know that I don't?" I was curious. I saw each dying person as a portal to another world. I wanted to know how to reach across the chasm of silence that lay between us and have a conversation.

Strangely, without all the usual props of life stories and drama, without a professional role, without words, I had the freedom to study. With their permission, I experimented with on and off body touch, music, song, prayer, and meditation. I watched their physical responses, which eventually I measured in a study with biofeedback and discovered that….oh yes, they certainly do know we're there and they were responding, at least on some level. I learned that the most important thing I brought them was my willingness to be taught, my respect, and my great curiosity. I learned that these most disempowered people had incredible power, even the power to help me find my own wisdom. How cool was that?

Later I would have a regular hospice job with pay and a long list of patients, paperwork, meetings, and politics. I would look around team meetings seeing lots of burnout, stern faces, lots of talk about regulations and medications. I didn't hear many questions, nor see many traces of the heart, though I know that somewhere in there my colleagues cared, but maybe had forgotten something important. Some had forgotten their own life questions and had too many answers. Most had pulled away from each other as colleagues. Mainly, I learned that the cost of losing our questions and resisting the gifts of the ones in front of us leads to disconnection, and that disconnection leads to burnout. I found that this "way of being" left marks on my heart and in my body that were hard to endure.

But don't despair. As teachers, each day we have the possibility of finding the most challenging, irksome student in our class and befriending them. Before entering the classroom, we can imagine them sleeping before us as an old person, or a newborn without language or identity, without the dynamics and problems we know so well. We have the opportunity to form a connection with them in their most primordial state, or just as we know them.

The truth is that whoever we are helping are at least partly our teachers, too. And if this is true, how are *we* doing in *their* class? Is it that they are not listening and sitting still, or is it that *we* are not?

What might change if we listened, questioned, received their gift of silence, or said thank you?

Perhaps the biggest change would be Us! And how exciting would that be?"

For the Preparation of Teachers

When you were young,
your eyes awash with wonder and delight,
your heart swirling with questions,
and your life seemingly far off,
waiting for you like some mirage on the far horizon,
there was a teacher whose path intersected with yours,
who helped you step into your being
and take the first steps on a journey
that has led you to this place.

As with all great teachers
they manifested a commitment to their calling,
spent years in rigorous preparation, devoted study,
moments of intense introspection,
and relentless practice, stumbles, failures,
but always a resilient tenacity,
a willingness to overcome fear and doubt,
to free themselves to be themselves,
to reveal their enthusiasm and joy,
and encourage their students to unleash their own spirit.

Their quiet work,
preparing in isolation or with their own teachers,
their exploration of the quiet places of the heart,
its old wounds and elemental fears,

has helped them guide you to break down the walls
in which you've imprisoned yourself,
and encouraged your first bold steps
on a journey you once thought impossible.

Bless the teachers who inspired you,
that set your heart to beating, breaking, and healing,
who saw your potential and your gifts
even when you were blind to them.

Bless the courageous display
of their own gifts and their flaws,
for by displaying the courage of their convictions
and showing you the face of their humanity,
they have given you permission to be less than perfect,
to come out of hiding and let your precious heart shine.

May you invite into your life the teacher you need
        at this moment.

May you dedicate yourself
to the practices, questions, and experiences,
that allow you to guide others on their journey.

And when you are ready,
may you humbly claim the honor
of being called "teacher".

The Pointer

The Zen teacher's dog loved his evening romp with his master. The dog would bound ahead to fetch a stick, then run back, wag his tail, and wait for the next game. On this particular evening, the teacher invited one of his brightest students to join him – a boy so intelligent that he became troubled by the contradictions in Buddhist doctrine.

"You must understand," said the teacher, "that words are only guideposts. Never let the words or symbols get in the way of truth. Here, I'll show you."

With that the teacher called his happy dog. "Fetch me the moon," he said to his dog and pointed to the full moon.

"Where is my dog looking?" asked the teacher of the bright pupil.

"He's looking at your finger."

"Exactly. Don't be like my dog. Don't confuse the pointing finger with the thing that is being pointed at.

"All our Buddhist words are only guideposts. Every man fights his way through other men's words to find his own truth."

For Colleagues

"If you want to travel fast, go alone.
If you want to travel far, go with others."

You share your journey with colleagues,
pilgrims who join you on the path
as you walk through familiar valleys
to the edge of unexplored frontiers.

There are times you travel together in silence
in reverence for the magnificent terrain that
     surrounds you,
not needing words to express your delight
at the glance of a student whose eyes show
the passion of a fire that you have lit.
Only those on the journey know this joy.
A nod of acknowledgement from a fellow pilgrim
is all you need to sustain you.

Late in the day you camp together by the black river
and speak in quiet voices of things you have seen
     and done.
You trace lines on well worn maps,
and those that have gone before
share what they know about what lies ahead.

On the darkest days,
when the classroom is a lifeless desert,
you turn to each other
for the nourishment of a kind word,
more necessary in the moment than water.

May you comfort your colleagues
who are on their own fearsome journeys,
and be the ear that listens selflessly,
never ceding advice unless asked,
seeking to understand before being understood.

May you walk past conversations
that descend into anger, frustration, and darkness,
for those that live in these stories have lost their way.

May you speak plainly
and directly with colleagues,
especially those with whom you are in conflict.

May each of you on the journey
navigate by some bright star fixed in the sky,
there for you perpetually, day and night,
far beyond petty personal concerns,
connecting you to the eternal,
always constant and true.

May you share the road with new friends,
and welcome them with loving embraces.

May you walk in the darkness courageously,
letting your light, light the way of others,
helping them when they stumble or fall.

On the day your paths diverge,
and you leave your colleagues,
called to travel a different route,
may you each have a deep conviction,
as clear as the North star
to guide you and keep you safe.

At the End of the School Day

Before they come to sweep your classroom
in preparation for tomorrow,
may you embrace the silence and look back on the day
asking:

What did I see reflected in the eyes of my students?
Did I allow my vision to settle on the one who
    needed to be seen?
Was I truly present to what was called for
    in those moments?

Did I neglect someone today?
Did I take time for myself?
When was I most comfortable?
What did I avoid?

What new thoughts came to me?
How well did I listen?
What moods visited me?
What did I miss today?

Did I cast my shadow on the students that needed shade?
Leave space for the shy ones?
Stake those that needed my support?
Let my sun shine on those that turned to me for warmth?

What dreams were created today?
Was I open to love?

Looking back,

Why was I given this day?

THE CHALLENGE

"Happiness is not the absence of problems;
it's the ability to deal with them."

STEVE MARABOLI

I believe teaching is a spiritual activity. I don't mean a religious activity but spiritual in the sense that when a young child comes to us, they come to us whole…mind, body and spirit. It's through their spirit, personality, heart or whatever word we wish to use to describe the inner world from which they experience life and learning, that they find meaning, connection, relevance, and inspiration. Without these things learning is merely a lifeless exercise of the mind and school can be deadening. When we teachers work with, and through the heart, (our heart and theirs), we bring our spirit to learning and thus bring learning to life.

As educators we're truly privileged to work in the "Garden of Hearts", which is how I look at the classroom. But working in this garden isn't easy. Schools have become institutions that have at their core the need to systemize and compartmentalize learning in order to provide an accredited and somewhat standardized education to millions of children at a time. The intimate, one-room schoolhouse has become a modern day super-sized agri-business, (and to mix metaphors a bit) with a factory-like approach to learning. Picture students moving from class to class as if on a slow moving Ford assembly line with content specialists adding their particular piece of the "educational car" to the student as they move by. Or imagine the teacher riding a tractor spraying fertilizer on thousands of acres of neatly planted rows of the same crop. How unlike a garden our institutional school system can be when looked at from afar.

But neither the agra-business nor the factory metaphor

is completely accurate because we have individual classrooms and in each is a teacher who has the ability to create a world or garden of their own. It's the heart of the teacher that ultimately determines whether the classroom is simply one more stop on the educational assembly line or a special place full of curiosity, exploration, inspiration, and discovery.

No doubt, creating gardens of learning that cultivate the minds and hearts of our students in today's environment is more difficult than ever. The political winds of the times have blown in like a storm. The call has been for more standardization, automation, more scripting, more testing, and more measures of accountability that omit the parts of learning that can't be weighed and measured on multiple choice tests. How hard it is for a teacher to buck the system and keep learning a path with heart.

Great teaching is much more like gardening than it is manufacturing or engineering. It's not possible, nor desirable, to build children to predetermined specs, no matter the blueprint, because each child is unique. Instead, we work in our classroom gardens to nurture each of them as individuals and strive to cultivate their innate gifts and their curiosity. The best teachers, like the best gardeners, know their students and are familiar with their needs. Some students need room to grow, some need sun, and some shade. There are those that require frequent watering, and a few that need to be staked for support; but one thing is certain, they're each unique human beings and should be treated as such. This is the art of teaching, the art of gardening.

A good teacher, working "In the Garden of Hearts", also knows themselves, for we can't connect, motivate, and inspire others if our own heart is closed or only partially open. To be successful we must bring everything we have, and everything we are, to the teaching and learning process. Whatever we'd like our students to learn must be brought to life in ourselves first. It's simply the way authenticity and integrity work and it's our authenticity that breaks through the tendency of many students (and their teachers) to "play school". Kids aren't dumb. They know when we're sincere and fully committed to them and when we're just fulfilling our role on the assembly line. If we settle for "playing school", so will they.

Perhaps the most challenging issue we face as educators is to help each of our students awaken to their own voice, power, and gifts. But how can we teach so many and still find time to nurture each of these special hearts? Time is precious and short and we're under tremendous pressure to produce academic results. It feels like there is no other way for us to teach but to give in to the current obsession with test scores and overlook the needs of the individual.

There are no easy answers, nor well traveled paths for the teacher who wants to do more than work on the educational assembly line. One thing is for sure, however; if we're to make a real difference in this world, and in our classrooms, it will be through the unity of our mind, body, and heart.

Teaching Grammar

I leaned over her desk
pointing out errors,
commas missing, run-ons,
tenses mismatched, confusing constructions.

She was a quiet one who sat in the front;
a timid rabbit in her warren.

My eyes rushed across the single, handwritten page,
heavy boots trampling through her delicate world,
my finger settling on a sentence
while I spoke to her in frustration.

A bitter teardrop fell blurring the blue ink,
and then another and another,
like an unexpected summer shower
they continued to fall,
her body heaving in silent sobs.

Her story of a pet's dying was crude.
I saw nothing but grammar,
the way an illiterate sees only strange marks on paper,
and in the tiny pond that formed on her desk
I saw my reflection,
and in it,
the shadows that darkened my own heart.

After a Destructive Encounter

Although we're professionals, we're also fallible human beings, prone to mistakes, intentional and accidental, that can hurt those around us, especially our students.

In my life I know
I've walked through the field of flowers
that is my classroom,
intent on reaching my destination,
not seeing the blossoms I trampled as I strode.

I know I've interrupted,
skipped over,
lost patience,
embarrassed,
cut with sarcasm,
intimidated,
turned my back,
joked at others' expense,
thundered loud and dark,
and most hurtful of all,
withheld my attention,
my heart,
and my love.

For each hurtful action, or inaction,
I am deeply sorry.

May I return to my classroom each day
committed to take more care,
to mend what I can,
to soothe the hearts I have hurt,
to replant and revive.

May I learn to forgive myself
and love myself as imperfect as I am,
for redemption and rebirth are possible at every moment.

May I sing the song that every child longs to hear,
for it is the song my heart longs to sing.

The Guest House
RUMI

This being human is a guest house.
Every morning a new arrival.

A joy, a depression, a meanness,
some momentary awareness comes
As an unexpected visitor.

Welcome and entertain them all!
Even if they're a crowd of sorrows,
who violently sweep your house
empty of its furniture,
still treat each guest honorably.
He may be clearing you out
for some new delight.

The dark thought, the shame, the malice,
meet them at the door laughing,
and invite them in.

Be grateful for whoever comes,
because each has been sent
as a guide from beyond.

For a Lack of Support

Teaching can be a knife's edge of confusion caused by any number of things: a student who has found a brilliant way to disrupt the class, an aggressive parent that has taken on the role of bully, a large and difficult class with a co-teacher who is incompetent or lazy, a teaching schedule that few human beings could manage without losing their minds, participating on a planning team that circles round and round and rarely makes progress. Need I go on?

Lost in frustration our heart cries out for help but sometimes those who can assist us don't. They keep their distance and drive by us like commuters passing an accident, happy its not them on the side of the road, glad to get past the flashing lights and commotion so they don't have to break their routine and be late for the chaos of their own workday.

A teacher once told me of feinting as the doors of the subway slid open on her commute to school. People, unwilling to help, stepped over her in their rush to get to work.

So there she lay.

Knowing there are people who can help us, and in some cases, are supposed to help, who don't, only adds to our suffering. We become angry and think,

"What kind of world is it where people ignore those in need?" "What kind of people are we?"

But eventually someone did come to help the teacher to her feet and stayed with her until a policeman arrived. And people do pull over at the sight of accidents to do what they can to help.

When we feel we're washed up on an island and forced to fend for ourselves while those around us seem disinterested in our plight...may we practice patience and compassion for there is much good in the world and most of us want to do the right thing. We simply forget from time to time.

May we have the courage to ask for help when we need it, and may we have the wisdom to look for help in the right places.

May we find ways to heal ourselves and sustain our peace of mind in the midst of rancor.

May we forgive the chairperson, colleague, or principal who plays favorites and ignores us, or changes their allegiance the moment a parent complains, or walks past a chaotic classroom...because whatever holds them back...whether it's selfishness or fear, is surely the doorway to their own suffering.

May we never forget to help others in need.

Assessments

Somewhere in the graphite smudge
on the printed test sheet
a child is buried
in a jumble of scannable answers.
But there are no measurements for life's eternal questions,
the ones poets suffer to grasp
lying awake, restless, in reflected moonlight.

It's no surprise to you that some answers
refuse to bow to the tyranny of bubbled rows.

But how often do we find ourselves measuring
who they are and what they're capable of,
our minds assessment machines,
creating stories about them,
assumptions upon assumptions,
this one, nice,
this one, trouble,
this one has had it hard,
this one has talent.

On and on we go
filling in the circles of our own private measure.

May we remember
that when we label our students we diminish them,

merely sketching a portrait of shadows
no better than the pencil smudge on the scan sheet,
which like the encroachment of darkness
obscures the possibility of discovering the true self
    they are,
and the hope of meaningful transformation.

May we remember that every day is a frontier of
    new choices,
each choice holding the potential of a new path
and a new life for each of us.

May we learn to work with each student
without preconceived notions, tabula rosa,
releasing them from the invisible prison of judgement
that we've constructed for them.

May we empty our minds and hearts of our assumptions,
allowing ourselves to be with our students in the wildness
    of the moment,
to welcome courageous encounters with the essence of
    who they are.

May we hold the space for the gifts within them to grow,
and maintain a ferocious innocence to meet them
    anew each day.

May we listen to others in order to be heard.

May we learn to see with the heart
that which may not be seen with the eye.

And no matter how long and difficult the journey
may we always find the way to love.

Holding

CHASE MIELKE

I have held a lot as a teacher.
I've held my tongue, comments and questions:
"Did you actually think that was a good idea?"
"Yes, there is such a thing as a stupid question."
I've held you after class.
"What's going on?"
"Are you okay?"

I've held my gaze of disbelief
Watching you walk out the back door
Only to return hours later, cigarette smoke
Sucking our oxygen as it
Drifts in your
Wake.

I've held ideas,
Beliefs about effort and intelligence
Beliefs about what I teach,
Why you should care,
Why I should care,
Why it matters.

I've held this thing called hope,
This thing with feathers, fraying and dry.
I've held it as its melody and song

Fractures with dissonance,
Notes to a different key
Than I wished you would sing
Time after time I search for our mutual melody.

It is in these moments when my grip is slipping
That I tighten my hold,
Knowing that although purpose is muddy and slick,
I can't let go of hope.
Of purpose.
Of meaning.

I can't let go of my belief that although
We
Are ships passing —
Our separate waves crashing and blinding
Our paths —
My mission is loud and bright:
To hold a path.
To believe in hope
In planted seeds and tangible dreams
To believe in you,
Even when you refuse to hold yourself.
Hold yourself back.
Hold yourself accountable.
Hold yourself higher.

I continue to hold.
I continue to hope.
Even when you let go,
I will tighten and endure
So you see
So you know
So you feel
What it means
To believe.

Sickness

Whether a minor cold or a sickness deep and debilitating,
each illness brings with it a raven's wing shroud
    of darkness,
eclipsing the routine vitality and constancy of
    the radiant sun.

Now, you pass through a veiled curtain
to a feverish world that is yours alone,
where you must dwell for a time, separate from others,
your universe grown small, your orbit turned inward.

The routine of life broken,
the health you've taken for granted a stranger now,
you find yourself in an unfamiliar valley,
walking a path that winds through new terrain
and places of the heart seldom traveled.
This is a place for reflection,
a chance to heal the spirit, as well as the body,
your illness much more than a physical state.

You may be surprised to find that even in sickness
there is a persistent ache of responsibility
for your calling and the students you teach.
But now is a time for healing,
a time to let go of obligation and the gossamer

threads of guilt,
for they feed illness.

May you bring your focus to the needs of the body,
and the requirements of the heart,
for there is an inner process at work that must play out
    in its own way,
in its own time.

Neither worrying nor thinking will bring the health
    you seek,
and just as the river runs according to the ways of water,
your body's turbulent complaint will unfold as it will.

Although you cannot control the flood of your discomfort
you can navigate it with faith and courage.

Understanding this is the unexpected gift
hidden inside every illness.

For Stress

Stress squeezes your heart until all that's left is a
    fistful of sand.
Someone tells you to manage your time more efficiently,
but time is not something that will bend to your will,
and those that live in hope that the world and our work
will get easier over time will be disappointed.

Pressured by our schedules we rush frantically
    through our days,
and toss anxiously through restless nights,
overwhelm and stress weighing us down,
causing us to fall even further behind.

We feel a victim of circumstances,
our bodies tighten,
our breath shallow,
as we spiral out of control in perpetual fight or flight.

Stress begets stress.
Our heads down, noses to the grindstone,
seeing only what's in front of us,
ignoring the long term, the big picture;
storing problems for the future,
simply increasing our burden.

No matter our circumstances we must learn a new
    way to live,

to abandon the chase
and the thought patterns and behaviors that weakens us
and threaten our health.

Stress is not a set of external circumstances
but a response to those circumstances.
What is severely stressful for one,
is an exciting challenge for another.

How we respond is in our control,
and taking responsibility for it immediately eases our burden.

Close your eyes and walk near the edge of the sea.
Let your footsteps disappear in the sand
as the ocean spills its caresses generously on the shore
gloriously displaying its relentless and unconditional love,
whether or not you're ready to receive it.

In this moment the sounds of a dozen sea birds,
descendants of a thousand generations that have
    lived in this place,
who know the winds, the tides, and vagaries of its weather,
rise on the shoreward wind,
sharing their excitement in daring swoops,
no thoughts of responsibility,
no lists of to do's.

May you relax into the mystery of this moment.
And let your heart soar with the terns
and the rhythm of the infinite ocean.

Helping the Student Who Has Suffered Trauma
DENNIS MOORMAN

Oftentimes, students who have suffered trauma will have difficulties in learning, due to a natural defense mechanism known as dissociation, where they disconnect from their own bodies so as not to feel the overwhelming pain associated with the trauma. Creating a safe and supportive environment can be an important element that allows the student the time and space to reconnect with self and relax so that they will be more open to the learning experience. When I embody this safety and support, other bodies will resonate with mine.

From time to time throughout the day, especially when I am feeling overwhelmed, I bring my attention to the physical sensations of my body. I especially notice the soles of my feet touching the ground. What is the physical sensation of my feet touching the earth? I take note of what is happening in my legs. As I bring my attention to my legs and feet, I notice that the energy in my body also moves downward. Where our attention goes, energy also flows. Now I notice where my body is feeling the physical sensation of support. I open myself to receive that support and notice how my body responds. As I feel ready, I notice where my body is becoming more relaxed. I take time to rest in that settled place within. I connect more deeply with the safety in my own body and I allow this grounded feeling to connect me with all beings that also have a need to feel rooted.

Avoiding Resistance
Dennis Moorman

When resistance arises, it is usually our body's way of protecting us from following a path that we are not yet ready to take. When I respect resistance as my body's natural mechanism for self- defense, I am freed of the impulse to break through it. Rather, I help create conditions which gently invite awareness of what is happening and allow the body to go to the space it needs in order to feel safe and free. When we feel that we have adequate time and space, a natural movement will occur which allows expansion at the rate at which we are ready to grow. Learning often happens best when our body becomes naturally ready to move freely in that direction.

Whenever I feel myself entering a space of constriction or resistance, I stop and notice my body. I become aware of the quality of my physical sensations. I don't seek to push through blockages. Rather, I gently invite my awareness to go to a place that feels more comfortable. I might notice if my body would like to make some movement. I can either imagine that movement or let it occur in a slow enough pace so that I can bring my awareness into every sensation of what is happening. As I do this I might like to notice what images or memories surprise me. Sometimes resistance can have a connection with a past difficult memory in my body. I honor this and give my body the time and space to seek out what it needs to find relief. As I enjoy the sensations of relief, I might find that the resistance in my body has also disappeared and I come to a new place of openness for curiosity and discovery.

Getting Unstuck
DENNIS MOORMAN

When we feel stuck and unable to move forward in a learning situation, it can often be helpful to move away from the place of difficulty to a space of well-being and competency. In doing this, we expand the sensation of power in our bodies, which frees us and opens us to greater possibilities when we revisit the place where we once felt stuck, so that we can see it in a new way.

At moments when I feel stuck, I pause and notice the physical sensation of that "stuck" place in my body, just for a moment. I then redirect my attention to a place in my body which feels more open and notice the pleasant sensations there. Or I might take a break and do something fun, which helps me to feel good and a greater sense of freedom. I let myself enjoy the pleasant sensations of freedom and fun and notice how the energy flows throughout my body in this new space. Then when I feel ready, I return to the edge of the place that felt stuck in my body and notice what might have changed. I realize that I can move back and forth between the stuck places and the open places in my body as much as I wish. When I do this I notice any transformational shifts happening which give me a new perspective and allow me to see new possibilities for growth and learning.

Hard Edges

When you were born,
you were born to both life and to death.
There is not one without the other.

The world can give you many gifts and yet can kill you,
cripple your body and spirit without a second thought.
And there is no guarantee that doing the right thing
will bring you success, or happiness,
at least not in the short run.

Doing the right thing can be an invitation to suffering,
but you do it because you know it to be right.

There is a hard edge to life.
There are people you meet and students you teach
who will hate you for no reason,
and there is nothing you can do to alter this strange
    chemistry.

Your heart breaks to see the suffering around you,
perhaps a student squandering their gifts in anger,
hurting only themselves,
slapping at your hand as you reach out to help.

Teaching's hard edges can cut you with precision,
yet hiding from its pain causes a deeper pain,
one poets suffer to describe.

May you live your own life,
not someone else's,
and if you fail,
may you do it with eyes open,
willingly.

First Year Teacher

You've done your part
and met them more than halfway,
but still they belittle your efforts,
or far worse ignore them,
disrupting everything you worked so hard to create.

Late nights thinking and planning,
lessons engaging and energizing,
fall lifeless,
blown away purposefully, maliciously,
scattered in the wind like dry autumn leaves.

As the days progress you feel a black hole of anger
begin to swell in the universe that surrounds your heart.
Resentment for their apathy and disrespect builds,
a steady pressure that invades every waking moment
and stalks the peace of your dreams.

Swallowed by this darkness,
seeing no way out,
unable to gain control or calm the storm,
your misery grows
and the shadowy contours of victim soon shroud
    your face.

No good advice can help you now,
your ship lost at sea,
tossed about in heavy waters,
a hurricane convulsing your heart.

To survive you must consider
steering into the fearsome onslaught.

It's you who must navigate the ship
amidst their endless bitter attacks.
It is you who must take a stand for your students
as well as yourself,
understanding that no learning
can happen in the midst of this storm.
Your only goal now: steady the ship.

May you calm yourself,
breathe through your panic,
and practice the confident voice
that has given way to shouting above the gale.

No longer will you absorb your students' blows directly,
feel them personally, or add to their power
by confronting them with sermons,
but rather step aside and calmly administer consequences.

It's here you must stay, day after day,
relentlessly turning into the waves
until little by little the waters begin to calm.

It is only when the storm has ebbed
that learning can happen.

You must survive.
You will survive.
Trust in this.

For Disappointment

We spend a lot of energy trying to avoid pain, suffering, and disappointment. But life has other plans for us. There is no way to live without encountering some amount of suffering and disappointment and oftentimes it's in this suffering and the breaking of our hearts that we experience new growth.

May the pain you feel,
the wound,
the broken vessel,
not result in a hardening of your heart,
but a softening
which lets the fresh light of healing shine through;
and with it an opening from which a different self,
familiar but new can grow.

Let your broken heart never close again
but be the source,
the fount,
the wellspring of new life,
and like sweet new shoots growing from a broken stalk
brilliant and vibrant,
spread upward to the loving embrace
and warmth of a welcoming sun.

The Smuggler and the Sheriff

In a system that has been captured by test scores and guarded closely by mandates, scripts, and the purveyors of accountability you are sometimes called, like the smuggler in the following story, to be mildly subversive. In order to keep teaching a path with heart, to inspire the hearts of your students, to bring learning to life, you must sometimes find ways to smuggle your unique gifts into the classroom. Be courageous, for you are the ultimate gatekeeper and the parts of yourself that you smuggle into your classroom may not bring you monetary rewards like they did for the hero in our story, but you'll reap great riches nonetheless...riches that are far more valuable than gold.

There once was a wealthy and prosperous city in the Middle East with a sheriff who was charged with keeping order and preserving the safety of its citizens and insuring that no unwanted black market merchandise ever entered the city. He was an intelligent, if somewhat pompous official, who thought very highly of his policing abilities.

Now in the same part of the country there was a man, well known as smuggler, who often visited the city. The sheriff wanted badly to intercept the smuggler, contraband in hand, and have him swept off to a prison cell where he would be no more trouble to anyone. Of course, there might even be a reward for having caught the smuggler in the midst of plying his trade.

The problem was, although he had a reputation for being

a smuggler, no one had ever caught him smuggling. One day he appeared at the gate with a single mule laden with sacks of worthless straw. The sheriff stopped the smuggler and searched his pockets eagerly, ran his hands between the sacks and the mule's back carefully, and of course, examined every piece of straw. Perplexed, he found nothing and reluctantly had to let the man pass.

A week later the same man appeared at the city gate again, this time with two mules laden with straw. The sheriff and his men, once again, searched the smuggler and his mules thoroughly. Once again, they found nothing and were forced to let the man pass. A month later the man appeared at the gate with six mules laden with straw. It made no sense to the sheriff. He thought,

"What's this man doing with his straw? It's worthless."

He also wondered how the smuggler had acquired enough money to buy six mules, but he found nothing extraordinary concealed on them and let them through the gate to enter the city.

This pattern continued for many, many months. Each time the smuggler appeared at the gate with a half dozen mules carrying nothing but straw. Each time he was searched, and each time nothing was found and he was allowed to enter through the gates. As the months wore on the smuggler's clothes, which at first were woven of the most common material, had become expensive silken garments. They were quite fashionable and adorned with many precious stones. The sheriff, who suspected that something was being smuggled, was understandably beside himself with frustration.

Over the years the smuggler became very rich and purchased a large home within the city where decades later, old and grey, he was visited by the sheriff, now retired, who was old and grey himself. He came to the smuggler's door filled with curiosity and looking for answers, for he knew at his age his passing might not be too far off. They both sat down at the smuggler's carved ivory table and a servant poured tea for them both. The sheriff was amazed at the extravagant wealth that was displayed throughout the house.

At last the sheriff spoke, "I must ask you my friend, how did you do it? I know you must have been smuggling something, something that produced the enormous wealth I see you've amassed over the years. I've examined every bag, every straw, every pocket of every person who ever worked with you and yet never found a single piece of contraband." He paused and swallowed a mouthful of tea.

"It's not possible that you fooled me. I have been as thorough as any man could be, yet I feel like a fool, because I have seen you grow rich right before my eyes and yet cannot explain how. Please tell me sir, what is the secret? How did you do it? Do not be cruel and let me go to my grave without knowing. As Allah is my witness, I beg you whisper your secret to me. Without it I shall be restless throughout eternity." With that he looked at the smuggler with eyes that were very sad and yet hopeful.

The smuggler took a long sip of tea, placed his cup

carefully on the white porcelain saucer, and leaned across the table towards the sheriff, who seeing this gesture also leaned in.

The smuggler smiled and whispered most gently, "I was smuggling mules."

After a Long Absence

Yes, you were missed,
for there were gifts
that only you could bring to your students.
After all, we teach who we are.

Your long absence broke the circle
that you, through the beauty of your heart, created,
and after a time the circle closed behind you,
and you were no longer in it.

This is the painful truth of a long absence.
It must be this way for life to move forward.

For a time you became a gauzy dream to them,
a cherished memory,
no longer present, no longer real.

Unlike death, your absence was not permanent,
but still painful to those you love
and who love you.

Allow them time to open to you again.
Know that a new and different bond must be built,
for neither they, nor you, are the same as when you left.

Be patient,
a joyful homecoming awaits.

Teaching What Can't Be Taught

Some of the most important things I learned during my years in school weren't found in textbooks or taught to me…at least not in the traditional way. Most educators agree that learning things like perseverance, compassion, and gratitude are important for children but they can't truly be taught via books, videos, or discussions, anymore than we can learn to play the piano by reading, watching, or talking about it, especially if we define learning as being able to apply our knowledge. So, how does a teacher go about teaching the things that can be learned but can't be taught?

The most powerful methodology we can employ is to embody the attributes we'd like our students to learn. If we want our students to show compassion it's up to us to be compassionate. If we want them to be risk takers, we must take risks. It's through the simple lesson of our example that our children experience what compassion, perseverance, or risk taking, etc. looks like in action. In my own education the teachers in my life that shared their gifts freely, were most centered in their demeanor, authentic in their presence, and connected to their dreams, were the ones who inspired me. Simply said, I wanted to be like them.

Of course, one can never be like another, nor should we be, but the attributes that we admire in others can always be found, dormant, within ourselves. The role of we teachers is to let our inner light shine brightly enough to illuminate the tentative hearts of our students, bright enough to drive fear from the shadows, and bright enough to light the path that shows each of them the way to their own light.

For those of us working in the Garden of Hearts teaching the things that can't be taught is part of our ongoing spiritual quest. It's the embodiment of "lifelong learning" the phrase I see in so many school mission statements. The more we perfect our hearts, the better people we are, and the better people we are, the better teachers we become, for as Parker Palmer says, "We teach who we are."

The difficulty is that "letting our light shine" takes a bit of intestinal fortitude.

> "Our deepest fear is not that we are inadequate. Our deepest fear is that we are powerful beyond measure. It is our light, not our darkness that most frightens us. We ask ourselves, 'Who am I to be brilliant, gorgeous, talented, fabulous?' Actually, who are you not to be?
> "Your playing small does not serve the world. There is nothing enlightened about shrinking so that other people won't feel insecure around you. We are all meant to shine, as children do…It's not just in some of us; it's in everyone. And as we let our own light shine, we unconsciously give other people permission to do the same. As we are liberated from our own fear, our presence automatically liberates others."
>
> —Marianne Williamson,
> *A Return to Love: Reflections on the Prin*

By the way, "letting our light shine" and embodying our values and inner gifts in no way interferes with teaching the things that are required by our profession. That's the beauty of it. We're not taking time from a classroom lesson to deliver a sermon on why it's important to be grateful, we're simply authentically grateful and show it. We're not developing lessons around compassion; we are compassion.

Not only does being the "living curriculum" not interfere with teaching the required subject matter content, it actually amplifies our effectiveness. No experienced teacher will argue with the premise that students work harder for teachers they admire and respect. Good teachers know that they earn this respect and admiration by being their authentic selves and by respecting their students. And by the way, it's a low cost educational initiative because the only textbook we need for learning "the things that can't be taught" is the body…meaning body, mind, and heart.

So, I thank the teachers who treated me with patience, kindness, and trust. I'm grateful for those that were encouraging, optimistic, and passionate. I'm indebted to those that listened to me, that cared about me, that pushed me to come out of my shell. When I think about them now, I realize that these attributes might not have always come easy to them, that they had to work at bringing their own gifts forward, just as I do now, even in middle age. I can't say that I've been wholly successful at cultivating all the seeds which each of them planted within me, but I remember how much I admired them for who they were, and I know that with grace I still have time to open to their lessons, to step up, step out, and let my light, and my life, shine brightly.

Good and Evil

AUTHOR UNKNOWN

An old Cherokee told his grandson, "My son, there is a battle between two wolves inside us all.

One is Evil. It is anger, jealousy, greed, resentment, inferiority, lies and ego. The other is Good. It is joy. peace, love, hope, humility, kindness, empathy, and truth."

The boy thought about it and asked, "Grandfather, which wolf wins?"

The old man quietly replied. "The one you feed."

For Technology

Technology changes things. Change can be disruptive and many of us resist it whether or not we completely understand why. Can we open ourselves to changes that empower our students and transform our classrooms? Do we step forward to be masters of the technology or does it master us?

We are curious by nature.
We tinker and create.
Our alphabet is technology.
Our language is technology.
They can be levers to move the world and our students,
but may we never worship or bow to the power
    they wield.

Technology can separate us,
allow us to live in bubbles of our own making,
multitask us to distraction,
seduce us into turning away from the world
to take up residence in the bits and bytes of our
    plastic screens,
mere extensions of the machines we create.

May we use technology to open horizons,
explore the universe,
connect with others,
amplify our creativity,

bridge distance and time,
and empower the weak.

May we keep our hearts open to the miracles it creates,
but remain grounded in nature,
the natural world's, and our own,
never losing sight of the mysteries and miracles
that surround us in this moment.

May we always remain poets of our own lives.

For Parents' Conferences

A mother and father's most precious gift is their child. Most would give their lives for their children. This deepest of loves comes from the very core of their being. Every day of the school year parents entrust their children, mind, body, and heart, to us. Nurturing them is an awesome responsibility.

Every parent hopes that we'll be the teacher
who recognizes the special elements of their
    child's nature,
encouraging the tiniest sprouts of possibility
to bloom in wonderful aromatic petals of color.

But each also has the expectation that if this
    is not possible
we'll treat their child with respect,
maintain their dignity,
and protect them from harm.

This trust has nothing to do with test scores.

Bless parents who work and cannot attend conferences.

Bless parents who can attend but don't.

Bless parents who are not far removed from their
    own childhood,

uncomfortable with their new roles as mothers
    and fathers,
and those whose memory of school
is one of failure, difficulty, and suffering.

Bless parents that have traveled here from distant lands
to make better lives for themselves and their children,
unfamiliar with our language and customs.
They make difficult sacrifices for their children.

Bless parents who feel the confusion and hurt
of raising a defiant and angry child,
those who are overwhelmed and lost
and look to us for help or a word of comfort or hope.

Bless parents blind to the shortcomings of their children,
prone to blame,
who turn their frustration towards us.

Bless parents that find it difficult to trust,
and those who feel they know more than us.

May we fulfill the hopes that every parent
has for their children,
and cradle their golden hearts in ours.

Things That Can be Learned but Can't be Taught

The master knows her greatest challenge
is to have her students learn the things that
    can't be taught,
things that aren't written in ink,
but imprinted on the heart.

To do this she must be both student and teacher.

To this endeavor she can bring nothing but herself.

Insults

*Patience under insult means not succumbing to anger, aggression
or despair when threatened. Instead, it means being mindful of our
reactions and emotional responses, and perhaps finding wiser ways
to respond. Pausing, even for a moment, before reacting to a difficult
situation is a powerful form of patience.*

Once an angry man insulted the Buddha. The Buddha simply
asked the man if people ever visited him in his home.
Surprised at the change of topic, the man answered, "Yes".

The Buddha then asked if his visitors ever brought gifts.
When the man replied, "Yes," again, the Buddha asked,

"What would happen if you refused to accept the gifts?
Who would the gifts belong to then?

The man said, "Of course, they would still belong to those
who brought them."

The Buddha then calmly and, I imagine, kindly said,

"In the same way, since I do not accept your insults,
they remain with you."

For a Difficult Student

*No matter how experienced and competent we are, eventually we
encounter a class or student that frustrates us. Our challenge may
be a disruptive student, one that knows how to get under our skin,
is disengaged, or even more troubling, self-destructive. Strategies
that we've used successfully in the past have no impact. Stripped of
an effective methodology for dealing with the situation our frustration turns to anger. We ask, "Why is this happening to me?" "What's
wrong with this student?" "What do I do now?"*

The classroom can be a summer field
ablaze with flowers of every color,
bright faces smiling in the warm sun,
each growing silently in the softest of breezes.
But there are angry and unforgiving faces there too,
betraying deep sadness and nameless pain.

Remember these faces.
They are yours,
each part of the mosaic that is your classroom,
and as such, your heart.

There is one who has been sent
to push you to the frontiers of your knowing,
where all you have learned thus far
is but a starting point for your new journey,
and the terrain you enter now
is wilder than any you've traveled before.

This difficult child, this painful gift,
who has brought you to your limits,
has been sent to teach you exactly what you need to know
about yourself.

It's in the terrain of your anger and frustration,
wandering in a desert of despair,
with no path to follow, alone and lost,
you must be still.
For it's only in stillness that you will find the lesson
you were meant to learn.

This difficult student,
this child that disrupts the flow of the singing
    silver stream
and clear waters of your classroom,
is calling out to you in great need,
using the only voice they know.

The anger of this student has deep roots
having grown in poor soil,
pushing courageously through the cracks in a neglected
    sidewalk
passed over by those too busy to notice.

Perhaps they have never danced with intimacy,
now pushing away what they crave most,
hiding their anger in indifference,

expressing it in defiance,
calling for you to reinforce their perceived shortcomings
with your own anger or indifference,
proving to them that they aren't worthy.

May you never succumb to looking at this child as a
    weed to be pulled,
but always as a plant to be nurtured.

May you remember that he yearns to find his own place
    in the world,
and he too is a traveler in new lands without a map
    to guide him.

May you look beyond exteriors to the warm heart that
    beats within her.
May you open yourself in new ways in order to recognize
    what she needs,
remembering your own struggles, doubts, and missteps
so easily forgotten in the fullness of your own life.

And in the midst of the classroom
may you teach what each difficult child yearns
    to be taught:
that they are worthy of love,
and may that lesson take the proper form,
whether it be the loving caress of discipline

applied with respect and dignity,
or whether it be a smile, a word of encouragement,
some acknowledgment of their humanity and yours.

This dark gift,
the lesson you had to learn has found you.
Now you, the gardener, must work the soil.
Enrich it where you can.
That soil being your own true heart.

There are no guarantees of success,
and you may never find the warm fire of her true heart.

But know that each of us is growing and learning in
    our own way.

Be at peace.

Lost

Confusion and questions are often the precursors to transformations of our being. So it is, that at some point in our careers we awaken to find ourselves lost. It's in this moment of fear and disorientation that we must trust ourselves and our own wisdom to lead us to the self that wants to be born.

When you feel lost and run panicked in pathless darkness,
caught in a confusing web of questions,
may you stop moving and embrace silence,
apprentice to its wisdom,
feel the silver threads of memory
and the spreading sunrise of the future,
not yet formed,
whispering together in this moment,
restless in the gathering day.

In this conscious stillness begin to recognize
that wherever you are is home.

May you stand quietly, patiently,
as your life steps forward
into the moonlit clearing and finds you.

Be courageous.
Don't run. Listen.
Let the questions come.

What wants to be born in and through you?
What do you need to learn to love next?
Why were you given this day? This life?

May you remember who you are,
certain of nothing but the holiness of your heart
and the truth of your imagination.

May you live the questions.

Winter

"In the middle of winter I at last discovered that there was
in me an invincible summer." — ALBERT CAMUS

The newness of the school year is gone,
the days grown shorter.
You awake in darkness and return home in darkness,
part of a familiar and elegant routine,
each day flowing into another,
broken only by the holidays
with their short lived excitement.

In this season of frigid darkness life retreats.
It burrows deep and hides from the chill hand
that hovers over the frozen earth like death itself.

In the harsh and lonely days of the earth's journey,
so far from the sun,
it's your true heart that must warm the classroom.

Beneath the the crust of ice the lively stream runs clear,
seeds and bulbs huddle under a frozen blanket of earth,
even the life blood of the tree seeks sanctuary
from the great north wind,
howling its icy threats in the deepest darkness of winter.

It's your heart that knows the constancy of the seasons
and keeps the hope of Spring alive.

It's your heart that sees beauty in the crystal frost,
the gale, the barren trees, and clear nights of the
    dark season,
and it's your heart that loves the light and explodes
    with joy,
as the first tender crocuses raise their delicate heads
and shout their silent ode to Spring.

A Ute Blessing

May the Earth teach you stillness
as the grasses are stilled with light.

May the Earth teach you suffering
as old stones suffer with memory.

May the Earth teach you humility
as blossoms are humble with beginning.

May the Earth teach you caring
as the mother who secures her young.

May the Earth teach you courage
as the tree which stands all alone.

May the Earth teach you limitation
as the ant which crawls on the ground.

May the Earth teach you freedom
as the eagle which soars in the sky.

May the Earth teach you resignation
as the leaves which die in the fall.

May the Earth teach you regeneration
as the seed which rises in the spring.

May the Earth teach you to forget yourself
as melted snow forgets its life.

May the Earth teach you to remember kindness
as dry fields weep with rain.

— ADAPTED FROM A UTE PRAYER

THE HEART

"The heart has its reasons which
reason knows not."

—Blaise Pascal

The biggest lies are the ones we tell ourselves. How silly to think that by avoiding the mirror of self-truth that our heart will fall for the ruse and turn a blind eye to the things we wish to ignore. How ironic to think that by hiding from our own truth our flaws are hidden from our friends and those we love, who of course see all the things we refuse to acknowledge in ourselves. The joke is truly on us.

Our heart feels everything. Nothing that happens in our lives escapes it's powerful presence. It does this without conscious effort. Since we live primarily in our thoughts we're largely unaware of the subtleties it senses and its omniscient emotional consciousness. If we navigate to the heart and listen to the echoes of its wisdom it seems to travel to us like the plaintive tones of the humpback whale through an ocean of memory, strange yet familiar. We may try, but find ourselves unable, to translate these strange sounds into words. What the heart holds for us are not thoughts or words but shape, shadow, sound…and feeling. It's a language unto itself. Or perhaps more rightly described, the heart foregoes language and is simply an exquisite knowing.

The heart is an ecology full of felt emotion, sensation, and mood, mixing together to create an atmosphere with its own seasons, currents, tides, orbits, and tempests. It's filled with light and dark, storms, droughts, sun, rain, and variations in temperature. It's the weather of the heart that enters our dreams and plays out so elegantly in our waking life. All this happens far from our notice, as if the heart were a distant moon casting shadows on us, reflecting the sun, bringing us its light even in the dark, it's gravity moving the tides of the oceans, and we, being mostly water, similarly moved. Only those who live with their eyes focused on the heavens discern the heart's mysteries and the truths of its enigmatic energy. Whether the moon of our heart is full or gone to blackness, absent from sight, or a tiny crescent of silver, it's omnipresent in some form throughout our lives.

One way to look at the heart's wisdom is to understand that nothing ever really escapes its awareness. Our heart is filled with everything we feel and have ever felt. Our heart is like an attentive spider at the center of an infinite web of delicate filaments tuned to the slightest vibrations. Even when we claim to have been blindsided by a particular life trauma, if we settle ourselves and listen deeply we understand that at some point we sensed the movement of a filament, not in our conscious minds but in our hearts. Somehow we knew and somehow we always know. This is the peculiar treasure of organic wisdom that is our spiritual inheritance, the special gift that each of us carries within us.

For teachers it's particularly important that we pay attention to the ecology of the heart and the slightest vibrations of the filaments of its web. For we work "In the Garden of Hearts" and like all good men and women who work the earth, we look to the seasons, the weather, and the stages of the moon, to guide our planting, nurture our crop and reap its harvest. It is through our hearts that we feel the hearts of our students, that we hear voices that are too fearful to speak, or voices that speak too often out of fear. It's through this language without words that we come to understand their yearnings, their sorrows, hopes, and dreams.

But unfortunately there's a widely held belief in the educational community that any talk of the heart is mere 'fluff', nothing more than a dreamy, unrealistic world of unicorns and rainbows. The educational practitioners who feel this way about the heart disparage those who bring feeling, emotion, and other intangibles into the conversation about great teaching. They want what they consider "concrete" answers and practical tips, not open ended solutions or, heaven forbid, even more questions.

Nothing would make me happier than to dispel the view of the heart as weak. On the contrary, exploring the heart is probably the most courageous act we can ever take. It's quite common and very easy to shut down our feelings, to dissociate ourselves from life's inevitable pain and suffering, its excitement, and from our own insecurity and anxieties. I know how easy it is because it was my modus operandi for a great deal of my life. To avoid even the possibility of a broken heart I gave up residency in its environs and lived almost exclusively in my mind, intellectualizing everything, feeling little. Of course living this way was not a great way to build intimacy and form relationships. Why? Because the walls I built around my heart to protect it from pain also kept me from feeling joy and love... for myself, and for others.

I may be wrong but I think men are particularly susceptible to dissociating from our feelings. My grandmother once told me about my Uncle Bill being brought to the emergency room as young boy and the doctor finding a ten pound tumor in his abdomen. He was wheeled into the operating room immediately and the doctors went about removing the strange growth. The operation was touch and go and my uncle, my grandparent's only son, lingered near death for close to forty-eight hours. My grandmother stayed with my Uncle Bill the entire time, never leaving his side. She prayed and cried, then prayed and cried some more. She had the courage to feel, the courage to be there no matter what happened. My grandfather on the other hand, couldn't bring himself to go to the hospital. He loved his son so much the mere thought of losing him caused him to shut down his feelings, to numb himself. He was afraid to open his heart to the greatest pain any human being can feel, the loss of a child.

I believe, contrary to what the naysayers think, that letting ourselves feel and dropping the ruse that we're "bullet-proof" takes real courage. Letting others see us as we are, not just the carefully constructed image of what we'd like people to see, takes courage. It takes courage and strength to have a heart of service, to do things wholeheartedly even when the odds of success are stacked against us.

It also takes a strong person to live in alignment with the values and beliefs that we hold in our hearts and not compart-mentalize them. How many of us know someone who prays piously in public at the synagogue or church on the weekend and acts arrogantly the rest of the week? To me the heart is the citadel of real strength and courage, not the deadening numbness of dissociation.

The popular educational belief that a teacher who opens his heart is one who indulges in false praise, avoids difficult conversations, shies away from administering discipline, or from calling out injustice when it's called for is a myth. A teacher with a courageous heart doesn't abdicate her authority, nor her responsibilities. In the blessing "Hard Edges" I write that in order to protect the tender shoots growing in our classroom gardens our hands need to feel as they work. Because of this we refuse to wear gloves. Over the years our unprotected hands can become calloused and our fingers gnarled. The paradox is that it takes toughness and strength to keep the soil of our classroom soft and safe…and for us to remain open and feeling to the end.

Whenever I get in discussions with cynical educators who believe the heart is 'soft', I think about Dawn Hochsprung, Rachel D'Avino, Anne Marie Murphy, Lauren Rousseau, Mary Sherlach, Victoria Leigh Soto, the Sandy Hook Elementary School teachers who put their bodies between a madman with an assault rifle and their students. These courageous educators weren't 'soft' or weak. They acted from their hearts…from their exquisitely heroic hearts!

Unfortunately, we stand squarely in the doorway blocking the path that leads to the resources of our heart. To access our inner wisdom requires that we get out of our own way. How do we do that? By putting less energy into avoiding pain, avoiding feeling. Our challenge is to quiet our minds, slow the churning of our thoughts, logic, and rationality; and when we're ready, turn toward our heart and our elemental fears and longings, not away.

It's there in front of our inner mirror that we have the opportunity to come out of hiding. We can stop lying to ourselves. When we do, we may experience regret, or the anger, sadness, trauma or shame we've so carefully avoided all our lives. We might travel through a stormy period of emotions that shake us to our very core. This is as it should be for we're unlocking the doors of our own truth. If we do this with care, in the end, regret, blame, shame, sadness, and anger won't scare us, cause us to shut down, or run off over the hills like frightened deer.

Exposing our fear, shame, and anger; and finally embracing them along with the goodness our heart holds, as one whole, is our true "becoming". It's a glorious and welcome homecoming, for we are one person, incredibly blessed and incredibly flawed and that's what makes who we are so unique and so wonderful.

With an acknowledgement of our humanness and our newly opened heart, we return to our classrooms and our students transformed. We're not perfect, but perfectly whole. This newfound wholeheartedness opens us to see the world anew. More authentic now, not tangled in a web of self-deception, our classroom (and the world) becomes our new frontier.

Our heart, lighter for having released its burden, will lead us now, whether in bright sunlight, darkness or dense fog. For the heart navigates best when it feels most.

Accountability

The journey between shouting "Fix them!"
to the whisper of "Fix me",
is an arduous pilgrimage that can consume a lifetime
or occur within a single breath.

As we move beyond blaming others,
and see that like spokes on a wheel
the turmoil that permeates our lives and our work
converges at the hub of our 'self',
and recognize that the life we live
is no more than a reflection of who we are
and the choices we've made,
may we feel the liberating power of accountability,
and move from victims of circumstance
to designers of our own lives and classrooms.

Sometimes it's difficult for us to see
that words of complaint provide no relief
as we wither in the bright sun
cursing the heat from the feverish midday sky,
while in the distance an oak tree listing like a
    caring mother
spreads shade over the jubilant waters of a
    refreshing stream.
To save ourselves it is us that must go to it.

May we embrace a new path,
owning each step on the journey,
deliberately choosing the stones
for the foundation of our new home,
and placing each with care.

May we find peace in the knowledge that what we build,
in our own way, in our own time,
is a manifestation of the wisdom of our inner teacher,
the truth of our heart,
the solid cornerstone of all re-birth and renewal.

May others look on what we have built
and be inspired to embrace the power of their own
    accountability
and the possibilities of their own lives.

May we cease cursing the gods
and instead go about the work we were sent here to do.

Inspiration

To bring learning to life we are called to bring
    our life to learning.
Only the wildness of our own heart can awaken
    the heart of another
and inspire it to find its own illumination.

To inspire is to breathe into,
and through our breath
to bring life to the yearnings and dreams of our students,
for this is the doorway to the sacred lands of inspiration.

Let us not wait to be inspired,
but seek inspiration everywhere and in everything.

We move among infinite skies spun with
    shimmering gold,
stars so numerous they're numbered not named,
each star mothering blossoming galaxies of its own,
orbits spinning in all directions.
Let this be our inspiration.

We enter classrooms filled with young faces as bright
    as the stars,
in orbits beyond our knowing,
on the way to places near and far.
Let this be our inspiration.

May the dyslexic that struggles to decipher each word
    inspire us.
May the shy one who risks her safety to share
    a treasured poem inspire us.
May the child that feels relentless pressure to conform
yet seeks his own path to truth inspire us.
May the physically challenged inspire us.
May immigrant children finding their way in
    a new land inspire us.
May the autistic, the generous of heart, the popular,
    the disenfranchised,
each of our students and their precious hearts,
inspire us.

And as we go about quantifying, labeling, and dissecting,
as we study and predict,
may we maintain our reverence and awe,
and never lose sight of the magnificence of that which
    we're naming and numbering.

May we preserve our curiosity and wonderment,
hold fast to a savage innocence and fierce fascination
for life's endless surprises.
This is the knife's edge of the master's path.

May we allow ourselves to be vulnerable,
and bring our whole selves to this moment,
to help our students see the most brilliant vistas,

and the largest context in the smallest details,
as our own wild reverence is communicated
    directly to their hearts.

We need not thunder from the mountaintop
to set the world ablaze with excitement.
We can inspire with a quiet voice,
if it's authentic and holds within it
the spirit and mystery of the galaxies, moons,
    planets, and stars,
and our place among them.

Surrender

Here at the edge of the day, as the sky ripens,
the first clouds ablaze, crimson in the rising sun,
you kneel at the entrance to the sacred well
whose water is so clear you cannot see it,
though you strain your eyes to find it.

It's here with eyes closed that you surrender to
    the moment,
letting your hands reach out in their yearning to feel
    the cool water,
setting in motion silent ripples in ancient circles
    before you.

It's in the peace of this quiet surrender
that you finally hear the music of silence
and feel it generously pouring forth its precious gifts,
the taste and smell of the sacred water
slipping through the cupped palm of your hand
    like the moment itself.

All your life you've given yourself over to reason,
    logic, and fear,
but instantly you know the time has come to
    surrender to your heart,
the benevolent voice you've quietly refused to follow
no matter the depths of its truth.

Surely there are times to persevere,
but the clear waters of the ancient well reveal
what your heart has always known,
surrender can be as noble as resistance.

Surrendering to life is not giving up,
but opening up.

Now, in the blossoming morning of the new day
you breathe out, and let go,
setting off in a new direction filled with possibility
    and peril,
bringing life to you in new and powerful ways,
and it's here that you courageously surrender to
    your dreams,
and your need to control things you cannot control,
heeding your heart's call to love unconditionally.

This is the day you will surrender to your own faults
    and failings,
to your dark side, and your light,
to your unique perfection, as well as you imperfections,
embracing with compassion the flawed human being
    you are.

As you continue to surrender to yourself,
may you let go of your intractable beliefs,
the lenses through which you see the world

that keep you from seeing the truth of
    your own experience.

And in this letting go,
may you free yourself from hidden agendas,
the need to manipulate and protect yourself,
and bravely engage the profound journey,
that is opening before you.

May you surrender to hope,
and feeling,
and truth,
and love,
and especially to life,
to its mysteries,
and all its possibilities.

Doubts

Sometimes we feel overwhelmed with responsibility and wonder
whether we're actually having an impact on the world. We have so
many students and they have so many needs. We're human and can
only give so much. We doubt ourselves and our profession. We think,
"Perhaps it's time to pack it in."

A young man went for a long walk on the beach one day. It
was early morning and as the coastal fog began to clear he
began to see hundreds, then thousands, of starfish washed up
on the shore. In the distance he saw an old man at the edge of
the ocean working animatedly among the tens of thousands of
starfish that were spread at his feet. It was as if all the stars in
the heavens had fallen to earth and landed on this beach.

The young man approached and watched the old man
bend, pick up a starfish and then toss it gently back into the
ocean. He did this over and over, stopping from time to time
to stretch his back and catch his breath, The young man called
out, "Sir, what are you doing?"

The old man stood upright with a starfish held carefully
in his hands, "As you can see, these starfish have washed up on
the shore. If I don't get them back into the ocean soon they'll
die."

He tossed the starfish in his hand into the water.

The young man nodded his understanding, "But there
are so many! Look!", he waved his arms, "tens of thousands of
them, as far as the eye can see. You're wasting you're time. You

can't possibly make a difference!"

The old man listened politely, bent down, picked up another starfish, and threw it back into the ocean past the breaking waves.

He looked at the young man and said proudly, "It made a difference to that one."

Imperfection

An elderly Chinese man had two large pots, each hung on the ends of a pole which he carried across his neck. One of the pots had a crack in it while the other pot was perfect and always delivered a full portion of water. At the end of the long walk from the stream to the house, the cracked pot arrived only half full.

For a full two years this went on daily, with the man bringing home only one and a half pots of water. Of course, the perfect pot was proud of its accomplishments. But the poor cracked pot was ashamed of its own imperfection and miserable that it could only do half of what it had been made to do. After 2 years of what it perceived to be bitter failure, it spoke to the man one day by the stream.

"I am ashamed of myself, because this crack in my side causes water to leak out all the way back to your house."

The old man smiled, "Did you notice that there are flowers on your side of the path, but not on the other pot's side?" "That's because I have always known about your flaw, so I planted flower seeds on your side of the path, and every day while we walk back, you water them." "For two years I have been able to pick these beautiful flowers to decorate the table. Without you being just the way you are, there would not be this beauty to grace the house."

Each of us has our own unique flaws. But it's the cracks and flaws we each have that make our lives together so very interesting and rewarding. You've just got to take each person for what they are and look for the good in them. Remember to smell the flowers on your side of the path!

Integrity

*Nothing builds trust and relationships like "walking our own talk",
but living in impeccable integrity, following our own advice, and
embodying our beliefs is not as easy as we may think.*

There is a wonderful story about a mother in India who takes
her son to visit Mahatma Gandhi.

> "Great One! My son eats too many sweets," the mother
> said. "He is putting on weight, and his teeth are in peril.
> Will you please tell him to stop eating so much sugar!"
>
> Gandhi looked at the boy and the mother and said,
> "Bring the boy back in two weeks."
>
> The mother left, a bit disappointed and confused, but
> returned with the boy two weeks later.
>
> Gandhi looked at the boy and said calmly, "Please stop
> eating sugar. It is not good for you."
>
> The mother smiled, but before leaving turned to Gandhi
> and asked, "Great One! Why didn't you say this two
> weeks ago?"
>
> Gandhi smiled back and replied, "Two weeks ago I was
> still eating sugar."

Integrity has as much to do with the little things in life as the big. If we value a clean environment but rush past a corner trashcan and shoot a balled up paper bag at it and miss, and keep going, then we're not living up to our own beliefs. We may say to ourselves,

"Normally I'd pick it up but today I'm late", or "It's just one small piece of garbage and there's plenty of other people's garbage blowing around the street."

Nevertheless, we're still out of integrity. Is it a big thing? No. Should we beat ourselves up about it? No.

But where else are we out of integrity? What other stories are we telling ourselves?

Fear

Fear is a signpost pointing the way to growth.
If you're afraid, you're alive.
But it's difficult to welcome this uncomfortable friend.

Fear gets stronger as we approach new thresholds,
edges, horizons, unfamiliar paths,
for what's new and unknown can set our imaginations
    to running wild,
leaving us frightened and frozen in place,
or in panicked retreat.

Fear is a powerful friend.
We must treat it with respect,
turn towards it,
honor the place of its birth,
even if that birthing be one of pain and suffering.

Here is the story of my own fear:
As a young man
I was bullied at school.
I didn't defend myself.
I felt cowardly.
Later, as a man, I still harbored the shame of the coward.
I found it difficult to stand my ground.
I was fearful and easily intimidated by strong
    personalities.

There came a time when I was ready to face this fear,
and my teacher suggested I befriend the young man I
    once was,
the one that trembled before the bully in the schoolyard.
So, I closed my eyes and asked the frightened boy
    that was me so long ago,

"What do you need to confront this bully?"
and the boy answered, "A friend".

I honored his answer and afterwards,
whenever I had a conflict with a boss that was a bully,
or was intimidated by a colleague,
I sought out a friend willing to stand with me
    and support me,
and that made all the difference.

Years later there came a time when I was ready to
    visit my fear again.
My teacher invited me to return to the schoolyard
    once more,
and visit again with my younger self.

I closed my eyes and asked, "What do you need to
    confront this bully?"
He answered as before, "A friend."
But another question surfaced within me unexpectedly,
and I asked it without thinking, "What friend?"

"You", the boy declared without hesitation.
"I need you, as you are now, to be with me when
the bully comes."

Now, when the old fears come to me like choking
gray smog,
ready to blur my vision and send me back to trembling
in the schoolyard,
I close my eyes, and there I see the man I am now,
standing shoulder to shoulder with my frightened
boyhood self,
and the bully, no longer sensing weakness,
turns away, as does the fear.

Some may advise you to ignore fear and just act.
Be careful, for fear, like pain, has a purpose,
and we ignore it at our own peril.

When the time is right befriend your fear,
for the answers you seek are to be found within it.

May you welcome fear as an old friend,
who you've lived with your entire life
and ashamedly hidden away.

It's a friend that's done her best to keep you safe,
but that safety has come at a cost,
and now you're heart beats with possibility,

and a willingness to risk more for the life you
    want to live,
knowing there are better things ahead.

May you step forward together,
arm in arm, united,
whole.

Surrender

One evening a young Buddhist priest returned to his cave after gathering firewood, only to find it filled with demons. They were cooking his food, reading his books, sleeping in his bed. They had taken over. He didn't quite know how to get these demons out of his cave. Even though he had the sense that they were just a projection of his own mind—all the unwanted parts of himself—he didn't know how to get rid of them.

So first he taught them the dharma. He sat on this seat that was higher than they were and said things to them about how we are all one. He talked about compassion. Nothing happened. The demons were still there.

Then he lost his patience and got angry and ran at them. They just laughed at him. Finally, he gave up and just sat down on the floor, saying,

"I'm not going away and it looks like you're not either, so let's just live here together."

At that point, all of them left except one. The priest said, "Oh, this one is particularly vicious." (We all know that one. Sometimes we have lots of them like that. Sometimes we feel that's all we've got.)

He didn't know what to do, so he surrendered himself even further. He walked over and put himself right into the mouth of the demon and said,

"Just eat me up if you want to."

Then that demon left too.

Weariness

There is a good weariness, a fruitful and joyful exhaustion after a long day of doing our best, using our gifts, helping others, and in the process fulfilling our life's purpose. We lay our heads on our pillows and say, "Enough for today." and entrust ourselves to a well earned night's sleep.

But there is also a deeper kind of weariness. A weariness of the heart.

> *"For longer than I can remember I've been*
> *Dredging from its sludgy underside*
> *Giving myself and my loved ones the leftovers*
> *Of a life occupied with endless tasks.*
> *The elastic of my life is so stretched out of shape*
> *that it doesn't snap back anymore."*

There is a weariness of mind that causes our thoughts
   to wander aimlessly,
or fragmented, fly off in all directions at once,
like tiny mental explosions of light,
and the muffled drums of this parade,
cascade through our restless nights,
only adding to our fatigue.

Sometimes weariness causes our thoughts to become
   thick and dull,
and we, depthless, destitute,
forgetful and inattentive.

There are ways to rest and renew our minds,
to feel our breath,
the simplicity at the core of life,
breathing, breathing,
slowing the endless parade,
the wondrous silence bringing peace and presence.

There is also a weariness of body.
When it comes, it suffocates us with dark heavy clouds
that fill every cell, weighing us down,
our muscles listless,
and we, numb, depleted,
vulnerable to lethargy and illness.

Resting the body takes care of its needs,
precious sleep raining over us,
gently cleansing and renewing.
And we sometimes rest in exercise,
or in the joy of creating,
or using our hearts to feel.

But the weariness of the heart is the deepest weariness
    we will know.
When our hearts flag our lives are out of rhythm,
we turn inward,
disconnected, disappointed, disillusioned,
so weak we're unable to sustain anger,
or respond to love,

living as shadows, hollow,
our inner light unrecognizable.

We can replenish our hearts at the river's edge,
among the scents of the forest,
watching the flight of a starling,
or a thousand starlings moving as one,
hearing the call of a jay,
lifting our gaze to the night sky,
and its velvet cloak of glittering diamonds,
the delicate crest of moon comforting us with
    its reflected light,
listening to waves breaking on ancient rocks,
observing the passing of seasons,
the awakening sounds of morning,
the evening gloaming.

All these things renew our hearts
as do poetry, music, and art,
magnificent, mysterious,
bypassing the mind,
speaking directly to our spirit,
the true language of rebirth.

A weary heart yearns to rest in the company of
    other hearts
walking the same path,
pilgrims willing to share the burdens of the journey,
and ready to carry ours if we allow them to be carried.

May we learn to rest in the love, gratitude, and affection
of others.

May we learn to rest from the demands we make
    on ourselves,
and from our self-seeking, and self-absorption.

May we feed our hearts with beauty,
and truth,
and clarity.

Isolation

One of the great challenges of teaching is that we do so much of our work in isolation. Yes, we are in classrooms full of children, but once we close the classroom door few see our struggles, sacrifices, and triumphs. Isolation can lead to feeling unappreciated and a sense of loneliness.

It is said that we are never alone,
that we travel with the energy of clear light within us
and a host of lights around us.

Today you sit shiva in an empty classroom,
a body whose spirit has gone to other worlds
leaving only the echo of joy that once inhabited it.

You feel the isolation of the artist,
canvases stacked neatly in an icy garret,
no gallery, no accolades, no following,
only the work itself.

May you reap satisfaction from your work for
    its own sake
knowing that your art is not manifested on canvas
    or paper
but in the lives of the children you teach.

May the winds of time carry the gratitude of your
   students back to you.

May you have the good fortune to gather
    the bountiful harvest
of your classroom at least once in your life.

Gifts

It's in the realm of gifts,
given and received,
that we encounter the bewildering alchemy
which reveals the essence of our true nature and theirs,
for our unique gifts are the embodiment and true shape
of our passionate hearts.

To bring our gifts into the world is to live fully,
    with purpose,
inspiring our students to awaken to the mystery
of their own innate capacities and all the powers
    they convey.

Too often we focus on what is missing and not on
    what is there.

May we train our eyes to see, and our hearts to feel
the strengths that lay hidden within our students,
the ones they may not see themselves,
and may we encourage them to surface,
to take their place in the world,
each gift another light to illuminate the darkness.

Your heart in service to the calling of 'teacher'
is a magnificent gift
that you offer freely to your students each day.

Be patient and allow them to discover and
    explore you,
unwrapping your humanity with childlike joy
    and curiosity,
and as they do,
may you allow yourself to see what they see,
for how they interpret your gifts
is their gift to you.

Imperfection

The amazing art of *kintsugi* symbolizes the philosophy that repair requires transformation; the pristine is less beautiful than the broken.

Kintsugi gives new life or rebirth to damaged or aging ceramic objects by celebrating their flaws and history. The Japanese word, *kintsugi*, means "golden joinery" or "to patch with gold". This technique transforms broken ceramic or china vessels into beautiful works of art by using gold with lacquer or epoxy to enhance breaks, and in so doing, providing an aesthetically pleasing and unique way to repair broken pottery.

Consider how we might live a *kintsugi* life, embracing the cracks and chips—bringing to light the scars that have come from life experiences, finding new purpose through aging and loss, seeing the beauty of 'imperfection' and loving ourselves, family and friends even with all our flaws.

Ernest Hemingway wrote in *A Farewell to Arms*, "The world breaks everyone and afterward many are strong in the broken places."

Kintsugi is a great metaphor for those of us on the hero's path, the path to teaching mastery. It reminds us to celebrate our journey by embracing our broken places, our scars and our wounds. There is no reason to hide our bumps and bruises. In fact, it's high time we acknowledge and appreciate them for making us who we are.

Bless our golden seams.

For Anger

Teaching is an emotional endeavor. The youngsters in our care present us with a relentless flood of individual emotions and we, being human beings, react with our own. Unfortunately, we aren't able to take a quick break leaving 25-30 children alone while we calm ourselves. We have to deal with our emotions on the fly.

Our blood begins to rise, interrupted by a student,
late again, entering noisily.

Teaching and frustration seem to go together:
two students battling for a place at the pencil sharpener,
or one without homework pitching a silly excuse.

Daydreaming or whispering in the back of the room
    can do it,
as can indifference, the relentless tapping of a pencil,
or simple questions that have been answered many times
but continue to be asked even when the answers
    are obvious.

And there is our irritation at having lunch duty amid the
shrieks of students
    which somehow substitute for conversation.

We get angry at parent emails demanding to meet
    before school
on the same day the principal wants to meet after it.

We're frustrated that the lessons we've crafted so carefully
    and earnestly
can be ruined by an emergency drill,
or the shouting of a nearby colleague unable to
        control his class.

Our students sense our frustration,
our bodies ready to explode, or implode,
our fuse short, mood irritable,
cynicism a tenant in our house now,
and they withdraw to protect themselves.

Their fear and hesitation only feeds our anger,
and our downward spiral moves faster now.

We strive hard to suppress our frustration.
We feel we shouldn't be angry,
but we're human and our feelings are real.
We try to ignore it all, to muddle through,
but the unpleasantness doesn't subside.

A wise man once said,
"My students think I never lose my center.
This is not so; I just notice it sooner and get back faster."

Our anger is caused by the obstruction of our desires.

May we sense it as it arises,
and learn to breathe and recenter ourselves,

three breaths, or one breath,
it doesn't matter.

May we acknowledge our anger in this present moment,
focus on its sensations and where it lives in our body.

May we pause and choose a different path,
and if our students see us pause, see us breathe,
perhaps they will learn to do the same.

May we choose to let our anger go
like a wild horse
vanishing into the hills.

———————————————

"Bless me, that I heal anger hurts in myself
with the salve of self-respect,
and anger hurts in others
with the balsam of kindness."

—PARAMAHANSA YOGANANDA

Apology

I'm sorry that I sometimes forget who I am,
and why I'm here with you,
and neglect to take time to turn my heart towards you,
to listen to what you have to say,
as you open the petals of the flower of your own heart,
tentatively, cautiously,
not yet sure of who your are,
or who you are called to become.

I'm sorry for letting this extraordinary classroom
and these extraordinary children,
become absorbed into the routine of the daily grind,
allowing myself to miss the amazing gift that they are,
that you are,
that teaching is,
for it is a privilege to work in this garden of hearts,
and to see the treasure within you begin to bloom.

As the haze lifts, I see that I've been impatient at times,
even, I'm sorry to say, sarcastic,
self-righteous and judgmental,
so sure of my virtue.

For this I am sorry.

No doubt as I walk this path there will be more
    apologies to come,
for it seems there's no way to live in this world
without bruising ourselves and those around us.

May this apology open the door to a new
    kingdom of caring,
for myself and for you.

It's taken a long time to find the road to who I am,
and now I reach out to share this journey with you.

Trust

We can see it in our students' eyes,
they want to try an answer but wonder if it's safe.

Hesitating, feet on the gas and brake at the same time,
the moment passes.
They look away.
No one dares raise a hand and the class sits in silence.

Fear of failure and ridicule haunt the moments after
    a question is asked.
How easy it is to hide amid the familiar confines
    of silence.
We know this territory well having lived in it as
    students ourselves,
but courage stirs just beneath the surface.

As teachers, we walk as strangers among them,
and must remember that our presence communicates
    more than our words.

We build trust by embodying it,
by becoming an unyielding river of patient compassion
continuously washing over and eroding
the hard rock of fear that grips them,
creating a new channel for the waters of respect
    and dignity to flow,

helping free their spirits from suspicion and doubt.

Trust unleashes potential and brings promise into being.

May our classrooms become sanctuaries where failure
   is not feared,
and the peace of trust,
and the thrill of learning,
fill our hearts,
and theirs.

Resentment

Without even realizing, it's easy to accumulate resentments and carry them with us throughout our days. Resentments gets in the way of seeing our students as they are. They're like a smudged pair of glasses making everything we see seem out of focus.

Two Monks and a Woman

A senior monk and a junior monk were traveling together. At one point, they came to a river with a strong current. As the monks were preparing to cross the river, they saw a very young and beautiful woman also attempting to cross. The young woman asked if they could help her cross to the other side.

The two monks glanced at one another because they had taken vows not to touch a woman. Then, without a word, the older monk picked up the woman, carried her across the river, placed her gently on the other side, and carried on with his journey.

The younger monk couldn't believe what had just happened. After rejoining his companion, he was speechless, and an hour passed without a word between them.

Two more hours passed, then three, finally the younger monk could contain himself no longer, and blurted out, "As monks, we are not permitted to touch a woman! How could you then carry that woman on your shoulders?"

The older monk looked at him and replied, "Brother, I set her down on the other side of the river, why are you still carrying her?"

Failure

Excerpts from "The Man Watching"

—Rainer Maria Rilke

"What we choose to fight is so tiny!
What fights with us is so great!"

———

"When we win it's with small things,
and the triumph itself makes us small.
What is extraordinary and eternal
does not want to be bent by us."

———

"Whoever was beaten by this Angel
(who often simply declined to fight)
went away proud and strengthened
and great from that harsh hand…"

———

"Winning does not tempt that man.
This is how he grows: by being defeated, decisively,
by constantly greater beings."

———

Masks

We hide ourselves and our gifts behind masks
    crafted to show perfection.

Bless our flaws.

May we see that in false perfection we deceive
    only ourselves.

Long before we wore the mask of teacher,
we sat like our students among the rows of desks,
and dreamed their dreams.

May this silken thread of remembrance
connect us to the wellspring of compassion.

Gratitude

True gratitude is the language of an open heart.
It is felt long before the mind processes or labels it.

The gratitude of others is not to be brushed away
with false humility nor self deprecation.
It's a golden gift given freely.

May you honor it and let it open you to the giver,
a beautiful embrace,
whether given in passing
or spoken with great respect and deference.

The words do not matter only the heart of the speaker.

May you learn to express your gratefulness when
    you feel it,
and may you feel it always,
letting it fall like rain to nourish the parched earth
and the hearts of your students,
who absorb each drop
and grow richer and more fruitful because of it.

THE HARVEST

"Giving is an act of generosity.
Giving is sowing a seed.
The seed will produce a great
harvest of fruits."

Lailah Gifty Akita

The turning of the seasons eventually brings us to the harvest. Whether we've toiled in the garden for many months or our entire careers, the harvest is a time to step back and enjoy the fruits of our labors. It's a season of gathering and celebration; nature's out-breath, a momentary pause before beginning the cycle of seasons again.

The school calendar is still tied to the natural rhythms of the earth which have always dictated the farmer's life; and so our students, whose labor was once needed during the growing season, leave us in early summer, a vestige of an agrarian culture long gone. And because of this tradition, the teacher who has tended his garden carefully, doesn't reap his harvest like the farmer in the waning days of autumn, but in the full bloom of late spring and early summer.

But the differences don't stop there. At the end of his labor the farmer can walk among shoulder high corn stalks or take a bite from the ripe fruit or fresh vegetables he's planted and cultivated. But as teachers when the last bell rings we stand alone in empty classrooms. The students we cared for so carefully scatter to the four winds like the seeds of a milkweed floating out of sight on delicate gossamer wings.

It's rare for teachers to experience the fruits of our labors because the seeds we plant ripen in times and places far beyond our knowing. The truth is, the growing season of a child is much longer than a school year. In a sense we're merely stewards of their young hearts cultivating and caring for them only briefly. But if we're vigilant and attentive we can celebrate the tiny green shoots that we've cared for knowing that our work has opened our students to new possibilities, experiences, and questions. We can see that we've helped them to grow towards the boundless gifts of the sun, earth, wind, and sky.

Sometimes we miss the bounty of our harvest because we aren't used to celebrating our successes. Often we're oriented to seeing what's missing in our students and ourselves, not what's there. We find ourselves moving from task to task without noticing the magic moments that are happening every day in our classrooms. It would help if we slowed our pace and retrained our attention to spend less time perseverating over flaws, and instead let it (our attention) settle gently on these fleeting, special moments. Only then can we see the garden and all the children in it for the magnificent place it is. Only then can we feel our hearts swell with joy for the good work we've done.

But there is another harvest for us to celebrate because we're both teacher and student and, if we've been truly present and open to it, our work "In the Garden of Hearts" has taught us a lot about ourselves. This is the grand harvest that longs to be celebrated.

We can miss this bounty because we think of ourselves as the one's doing the teaching and our students as doing the learning. In fact our students have much to teach us if we're open to learning. Our classrooms can be wonderful mirrors of the self we are. They can be places that are true tests of our values, beliefs, and character.

Many years ago one of my most difficult students, Tim, taught me about the limits of my power and authority as 'teacher'. I expected him to learn because of my dedication, my commitment to having him learn, and the relentless effort I put in to make it happen. But I hadn't yet realized the crucial role Tim had to play in the process. In short, I couldn't force Tim, or anyone for that matter, to learn something if they didn't want to. I didn't like this lesson when Tim taught it to me. I was angry; but in hindsight, it made me a much better teacher.

Teaching can be like lighting a fire. Our match needs dry tinder in order to ignite the flame of learning in another. It's up to us to find the tinder. Even then there are no guarantees of success because real learning happens in its own way, in its own time, whether it fits in with our desires, or our timeframe, or not.

As students of our own lives we've been rewarded many times over for our work because the teacher's journey…the hero's journey, has helped us to grow as professionals and as human beings. We celebrate our personal and professional harvest with the knowledge that when the seasons change and we return to our classroom gardens again in the Fall, we'll be much better prepared to cultivate the young hearts awaiting us.

As we look back on the work we've done during this school year (or our careers) may we treasure the heroic steps in darkness we've taken to bring us to this place, and appreciate our contributions to awakening the voices of our students, cultivating their gifts, and setting them on the path to their own heroic journeys.

Yes, we are blessed to work "In the Garden of Hearts".

May we remember that our labors have not gone unnoticed by our students even if they haven't yet acquired the capacity to acknowledge our work or express their gratitude.

Our gifts are rooted firmly in their hearts.

Blessing for a Garden

Bless this classroom garden,
and the hands that plant, water, and weed.

Give us patience to tend our garden with care
and eyes to see the beauty revealed here.

Bless all who visit here;
may it give them joy.

May we grow,
day by day,
in grace, compassion, and love.

A Call to Live Everything
JOHN O'DONOHUE

One of the sad things today is that so many people are frightened by the wonder of their own presence. They are dying to tie themselves into a system, a role, or to an image, or to a predetermined identity that other people have actually settled on for them. This identity may be totally at variance with the wild energies that are rising inside in their souls. Many of us get very afraid and we eventually compromise. We settle for something that is safe, rather than engaging the danger and the wildness that is in our own hearts. We should never forget that death is waiting for us. A man in Connemara said one time to a friend of mine, 'Beidh muid sínte siar,' a duirt sé, 'cúig mhilliúin blain déag faoin chré' – We'll be lying down in the earth for about fifteen million years, and we have a short exposure.

I feel that when you recognize that death is on its way, it is a great liberation, because it means that you can in some way feel the call to live everything that is within you. One of the greatest sins is the unlived life, not to allow yourself to become chief executive of the project you call your life, to have a reverence always for the immensity that is inside of you.

—Excerpt from *Walking on the Pastures of Wonder:*
John O'Donohue in conversation with John Quinn

Beginner's Mind

Beginner's mind is a well known concept in Eastern philosophy and in many martial arts. It refers to having an attitude of openness, eagerness, and lack of preconceptions when studying a subject, especially when studying at an advanced level. Remembering the humbling confusion of being a beginner is important for those of us that teach. It imbues us with compassion for the children in our classes who experience that same confusion and feeling of being lost.

The great masters work hard to maintain
what they call the "beginner's mind",
an innocent curiosity common in our childhood,
so easily lost to experience and habit.

Familiarity makes the roads we travel each day mundane,
and it's easy to take our students for granted,
for them to become no more than objects,
as we go about the rutted routines of our busy days.

The beginner's mind is the learner's mind,
present in the moment and open to possibility.

The beginner shakes off the the dust
that has settled on their thoughts and actions,
to find something new within them,
to abandon the icy prison of well practiced expertise,
and awaken to the brilliant, wild conversation
    that is our life.

The innocent beginner knows no boundaries,
and small successes are amplified
by having experienced repeated failure
on the way to new learning.

May we welcome the joy of learning,
whether it be deepening an understanding of
    something familiar,
or discovering it for the first time.

The path of the beginner leads to wisdom,
and we are most alive when we are on it.

For Celebration and Joy

In the vast fields of your classroom,
bounded only by your imagination and theirs,
let your heart sing with the simple exhilaration
of being here on this glorious day,
blessed to wear a majestic multicolored cloak
woven from the smiles of the students you teach.

Permit yourself to rejoice in the knowledge
that within each mysterious heart
lies a surprise waiting to be discovered,
a gift overlooked now surfacing,
an explosion of brilliant radiance so bright
it casts a shadow on the sun,
and you, perhaps a catalyst, or simply a fortunate witness,
blessed to greet its emergence.

Today you feel the joy and clarity of good work
done for the right reasons,
and gaze upon your reflection
awash with amazement and delight,
dancing in the waters of the holy well,
fed by an ancient and eternal spring.

May you celebrate the triumph of all gardeners,
knowing the seeds you have carefully planted are safe
in the rich soil of the hearts of your students,

ready to germinate at the appropriate time,
a glorious moment of birth or re-birth,
as each becomes what they were meant to be,
a gift to themselves and to the world.

May you dance in the firelight,
sing jubilantly in star light,
and rejoice in the richness of the harvest.

Teachers Wanted: Must Love Students
From *The New York Times* Editorial/Letters Page

May 4, 2007

To the Editor:

We travel around the country helping urban and rural high schools increase college enrollment rates for economically disadvantaged students. The principals and administrators we meet say that what they need are teachers who love students.

Yes, they admit, a teacher needs the most sophisticated tools and curriculums, as well as expertise in psychology, neuroscience, pedagogy, learning differences, and academic standards. But it is the teacher who has the greatest capacity to care and to connect with the students who makes the biggest difference.

One Buffalo school principal said, "The school district cannot mandate what matters, and what matters most is the ability to love the students."

Where do we find such teachers, and how can schools of education deliberately begin to cultivate their students' souls?

—Keith W. Frome, Buffalo, May 1, 2007

The writer is the national director of education for College Summit, a non-profit group.

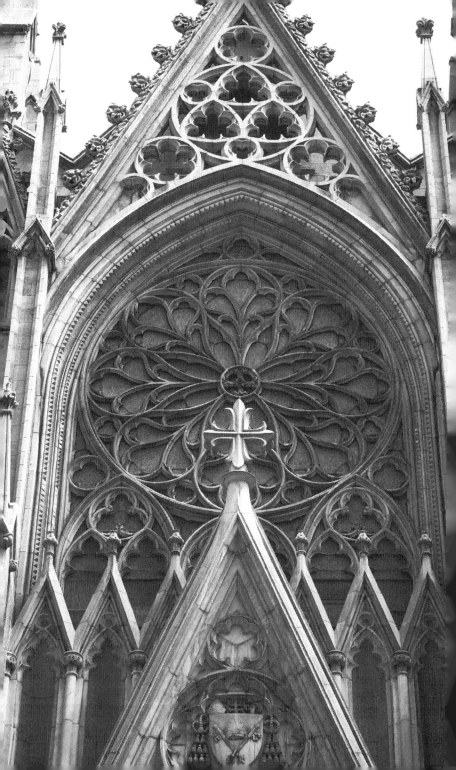

The Stories We Live In

*As teachers it's easy to become disillusioned with the state of
education and to feel wholly disempowered. We're overwhelmed
with responsibilities, mandates, and what we may feel are frivolous
and time consuming new initiatives. Changing our circumstances
may be difficult, but we can always change the story we have about
our circumstances.*

Our lives are stories of our own making,
and we cast ourselves in roles that we have written,
playing parts that we have chosen.

Often we live inside that narrative.
It can be a small world following a script
    someone else has written,
acting rather than living,
playing teacher rather than being teacher.

Like the old story of three men chipping stones,
one, dejected, seeing only the stone in his hand,
and the enormous pile, yet to be worked, beside him,
another imagining no more than a wall,
the third living in the story and the glory
of his role in building a magnificent cathedral.

May we learn to connect our lives to a larger story.

May it tell of Spring's cleansing rains
with their promise of new life and new learning,

Summer's warm days filled with excitement and gratitude,

And autumn's slowing,
reminding us to appreciate the last embers
of the burning passion that is our calling.

May we remember the dark story
of walking through the cold winds of winter,
it's icy breath having stripped away all
that was not essential to our survival.

Our story can have us in its grip or we can have it in ours.

May we learn to pause, step back, look up, and
        search within
to create a new narrative,
one as large as the universe;
for we're no longer satisfied with bit parts,
written by others,
playing victims, villains, martyrs, and cowards.

May we finally have the courage
to use our voice to speak our granite truth,
to step into the wonder and greatness of our true self,

finally the hero of our own life,
in our own classroom,
with our own students.

It's our story to write.
Our narrative to choose.
Our life to live.

Celtic Prayer

I arise today
through the strength of heaven, light of sun,
Radiance of moon,
Splendor of fire,
Speed of lightning,
Swiftness of wind,
Depth of sea,
Stability of earth,
Firmness of rock.

Being Human in the Classroom

At the center of the green valley that is your heart
there is a sacred well,
and if you come to it and empty yourself,
you will see reflected a familiar stranger who
    knows you well
and has watched your courageous struggle,
and waited patiently for your arrival.

The path that led you here,
winding among places unknown,
has brought you home to your self,
in your own way,
in your own time.

Long after the intricacies of mathematics and
    science have faded,
the excitement of words,
and the long tail of history are left behind,
who you are,
the breath of life itself,
will remain.

Each day holds the wild promise of new learning,
unscripted moments that can alter lives,
theirs, or yours,
for you are the 'living curriculum'

teaching curiosity by being curious,
courage through courageousness,
and the beauty of your humanity
by making mistakes in full view of all.

With your gifts on full display,
your frailties no longer hidden,
you give permission to your students to step
    out of the shadows,
into the fearless sunlight that you've set free
in your classroom and the world,
to embrace their own imperfections,
their own truths,
and their own humanness.

Every child born to this life has but one desire:
to be loved as they are.

May you learn to embody the love you are.

May you be the voice of unconditional love
    when you speak,
and love in action in all that you do.

Where the Answers Live

There is an old Irish tale of a young farmer, Brian O'Donnell, who while out walking on a dark Samhain night (October 31st) heard music from a fairy fort in a field near his cottage. He walked towards the feint music and as he got closer he found an opening leading to a tunnel. In he went following the music down, down, down…traveling into the very heart of the fairy fort.

Eventually he came to a point where he could see two old fairy women in front of a roaring fire speaking excitedly about a human girl who the Trooping fairies were bringing home with them so they might have a night's sport. Brian was very afraid but knew that the if he did nothing this human girl might never see her family again, so he waited outside the fort and when the Trooping fairies returned and began to pass near him he jumped out and grabbed the girl. Up, up the tunnel he went, running as fast as the wind. The fairies were angry and upset and chased after him. Just before leaving the fairy fort, one of the fairies reached out and slapped the young girl on the face and she was struck dumb.

Brian took her home and cared for her knowing nothing about her – not her name, where she was from, nothing. For a whole year Brian looked after and cared for the girl who never managed to utter a single sound. He didn't know what to do. He knew that if he did nothing the girl would remain dumb. In his heart he knew he had to do something to help her.

He trembled at the thought but he sensed that maybe if he returned to the tunnel in the fairy fort he might find some clue as to what to do. So as fearful as he was, on the next Samhain night, down, down, the dark tunnel he went again, his heart beating loud as a drum, beads of sweat on his fearful brow.

At last he observed the same two old Fairy women in front of the fire. One said, "Remember last year that mongrel O'Donnell took the girl from us and wrecked a great night's entertainment?"

"Wasn't it great the way we gave her the fairy slap and struck her dumb. Now she can't tell him anything and he's stuck with her forever." answered the other.

"If only he knew that three mouthfuls out of that bowl sitting there on the table and he'd have plenty of talk from her".

Without a moment's hesitation Brian rushed forward, grabbed the bowl, and ran like the wind up the tunnel, out of the Fairy fort, and down the hill to his home. He slammed door and waited with his heart pounding but the Fairies never followed.

The next morning he had the young girl eat three mouthfuls out of the bowl and sure enough she was able to speak.

"Brian O'Donnell you're a good man. You rescued me from the fairies, looked after me for a whole year even though I couldn't speak, and you risked your life to get me a cure and I thank you. But my heart is weak for my family who must be beside themselves wondering what has become of me."

"Don't you worry" said Brian "we'll head off this very morning to reunite you with them."

They walked for two long days and as the sun began to set on the second day they arrived at her home – and when her father who thought she was lost to him forever-saw her he passed out with shock. When they revived him they told him what had happened and he said –

"Brian O'Donnell you are a giant amongst men. I can see you and my daughter have grown close. I give you my blessing to be married." And so they were.

Buried within this little tale is the key to many of life's challenges. While it's human for us to look for answers to our problems outside ourselves, most often what we seek lies within us. We like Brian must return to the dreaded tunnel in the fairy fort and face our fears. This is where Brian eventually finds his solution... by turning into his fear rather than running from it. So it is for us.

The Golden Wake

"The boat is coming to take me home because I have failed in my studies here at the monastery," said the boy to his teacher.

"What can I say to my family?"

"Say that you did your best and that is as much as anyone can do," answered the teacher.

"But I wanted to be a famous monk and teach others."

"You can."

"How?" asked the sad boy.

"Live from your heart. I will show you. Do you see that boat making its way across the lake with the sun setting behind it?"

"Yes."

"Do you see its wake spreading across the lake? See how the boat looks like the apex of a golden triangle as the wake fans out from its bow."

"Sort of."

"Squint," said the teacher.

"That boat is you as you leave the monastery. The lake is your life. The wake is the effect that you will have on the world. Each ripple triggers another ripple, which triggers another. By constantly striving to live as wise and loving of a life as you can, you can teach the path of love to everyone you meet simply by being yourself; a few of these people will pass on your good example to others. Thus the expanding golden wake of good works begets other good works. Most important, notice how each ripple catches the sun and bounces its light back to heaven…"

As teachers it's good to remember that who we are, the self we are, carries more power than what we teach. We are the 'living curriculum' and we leave a golden wake behind us.

Classroom Leadership

As teachers we don't always think of ourselves as leaders. After all we and our students are at the bottom of the educational food chain. Often the curriculum, pedagogy, and pacing of learning is decided by authorities that seem distant and detached from the reality that we and our students face on a daily basis. Feeling disempowered, those of us who strive to be leaders take on responsibilities outside our classrooms on committees, as coaches, and advisors. But leadership is more than that.

Our students' hearts yearn to be led,
to where, and for what reason,
they might not know,
and to be sure, they may be unaware.

Sometimes we confuse leadership
with power, rank, and authority,
but a true leader stirs passion and commitment
regardless of their position.

Leaders lift other's vision to higher sights,
opening possibilities and revealing horizons,
making what seems impossible, possible,
empowering others to live richer lives.

There is a powerful leader within you.

When we fail proudly in front of our students,
acknowledge a mistake,
or offer a heartfelt apology,
we lead.

Taking a risk,
stepping out of our comfort zone,
sharing our passion and idealism,
laughing at ourselves,
is leading.

Creating context for what we teach,
connecting a single line in a poem,
an abstract mathematical formula, scientific fact,
the curve of history, the music of art,
or the value of manual labor,
to the greater universe,
or to a larger cause, a selfless purpose,
brings students to the edge of lands they never imagined.
This is leading.

Leaving the safety of our hiding places,
stepping forward into the hot light,
no longer an avatar or manicured Facebook image,
but an authentic human being,
with gifts and flaws,
is leading.

Embracing our own accountability and power,
forgiving those that need forgiving,
and engaging ourselves along with our students,
is leading.

Sharing our light,
helping students along the path that rises and falls
    before them,
supporting them when they falter,
bringing them to the mysterious fountain of
    their own gifts,
and encouraging them to peer deep into the clear water
to see talents hidden or avoided,
is leadership.

None of this can be done with a closed heart.

Peace of Mind

Once Buddha was walking from one town to another town with a few of his followers. While they were traveling, they happened to pass a lake. They stopped there and Buddha told one of his disciples,

"I am thirsty. Do get me some water from that lake there."

The disciple walked up to the lake. When he reached it, he noticed that some people were washing clothes in the water and, right at that moment, a bullock cart started crossing through the lake. As a result, the water became very muddy, very turbid. The disciple thought,

"How can I give this muddy water to Buddha to drink! So he came back and told Buddha, The water in there is very muddy. I don't think it is fit to drink."

After about half an hour, again Buddha asked the same disciple to go back to the lake and get him some water to drink. The disciple obediently went back to the lake. This time he found that the lake had absolutely clear water in it. The mud had settled down and the water above it looked fit to be had. So he collected some water in a pot and brought it to Buddha.

Buddha looked at the water, and then he looked up at the disciple and said,

"See what you did to make the water clean. You let it be ... and the mud settled down on its own and you got clear water... Your mind is also like that. When it is disturbed, just let it be. Give it a little time. It will settle down on its own. You don't have to put in any effort to calm it down. It will happen. It is effortless."

What did Buddha emphasize here? He said, "It is effortless." Having 'peace of mind' is not a strenuous job; it is an effortless process. When there is peace inside you, that peace permeates to the outside. It spreads around you and in the environment, such that people around you start feeling that peace and grace.

Tao Te Ching
LAO TZU

A good traveler has no fixed plans
and is not intent upon arriving.
A good artist lets his intuition
lead him wherever it wants.
A good scientist has freed himself of concepts
and keeps his mind open to what is.

Thus the Master is available to all people
and doesn't reject anyone.
He is ready to use all situations
and doesn't waste anything.
This is called embodying the light.

What is a good man but a bad man's teacher?
What is a bad man but a good man's job?
If you don't understand this, you will get lost,
however intelligent you are.
It is the great secret.

A Blessing for All Teachers

Bless the restless spirit of teachers
who walk through the moonless night,
stumbling as they follow
the mysterious and rugged paths of learning,
their lanterns lighting the way
for those students who choose to follow.

Bless the teachers who beckon us from our
    darkest hiding places,
destroying familiar touchstones and landmarks,
forcing us to find our own way,
to live our own life,
navigating by the simple truth
and clarity of our heart.

Bless the counselor teachers who sit at the
    courts of power
whispering words of compassion and mercy
to powerful kings and potentates,
who see nothing beyond themselves
and the halls of their kingdoms.

Bless teachers that lift us with their ascendent spirits,
those that invite suffering if it bring understanding,
those that teach with the example of their own lives

whether glorious and acclaimed or unknown and
   unresolved,
and teachers who plant seeds that they'll never
   see blossom.

Bless the healer teachers that live in caves and on
   mountaintops,
in small villages on the edge of lost rivers,
surrounded by the infinite incarnations of nature,
who know the mysteries of the forest and the
   secrets of plants,
passed down to them through the generations.

Bless those teachers surrounded by books,
those that create space for our answers,
and those that see our gifts,
and encourage them to come forth
even as we deny them,
in our fear and shame.

Bless the great teachers: Life, Death, and Love,
the deep sorrow that teaches us compassion
   and gratitude,
triumphs that reveal to us the hollowness of victory,
great adversaries that teach us of the limits of power,
and the painful lessons of war,
learned again and again by each generation

Bless our own teacher,
the one who loves us so well,
who sits quietly in the noise of our lives,
and waits for us so patiently,
the one who whispers to us in the moments before dreams,
for it's this voice,
unmoved by fear and self-deception,
that reveals to us
all things.

Hold On
PUEBLO VERSE

Hold on to what is good
even if it is a handful of earth.
Hold on to what you believe
even if it is a tree which stands by itself.
Hold on to what you must do
even it is a long way from here.
Hold on to life
even when it is easier letting go.
Hold on to my hand
even when I have gone away from you.

What a Ride!
DR. PATRICK B. AWOSOGBA, SR.

Lucy watched as class after class of students joyfully rushed out of the building at the end of the day. As they left, a few ambled over to the smiling principal to wish her a good evening, and then like the others, they disappeared onto the busy sidewalks of the South Bronx. Lucy took a deep breath and was filled with a sense of pride and accomplishment. Her mind drifted back to her youth in Lagos, Nigeria.

"What a ride!" she thought to herself. As a twelve year old Lucy had to support herself and to do so worked twelve hours a day, six days a week. A twelve year old working in Nigeria wasn't unusual because child labor laws weren't enforced. But Lucy had a secret gift. She was raised to believe in her capacity to achieve anything she strove for. When others faltered and lost hope she forged on. Her positive attitude about life and her belief in herself was what sustained her throughout the bumpy ride of life.

Lucy walked through the silent halls to her office. As she sat behind her desk, she allowed herself to relive those early days. She remembered the day she left home. It was cloudy that day but with no rain in sight. Despite the clouds and dense fog, it was unusually humid.

She'd been dreaming about this journey for a long time. Over the years she worked to get a good education and eventually juggled careers with a Masters of Business Administration and a degree in Econometrics. By all measures she was a success. But Lucy had other plans. She had a life-long dream to become a teacher. She smiled to herself as she remembered how excited she was on the day she was to board the bus and begin this new journey. "What a ride!" she thought.

Lucy was determined to bring knowledge and opportunity to others. So, despite not knowing where the ride would lead, and despite the unusual weather, Lucy boarded the bus and got acquainted with the other passengers. She and her fellow passengers shared pleasantries and expressed their excitement about the road ahead. Some of the passengers had doubts about the journey. They were afraid. But Lucy was excited to begin regardless of the distance, and despite the challenges. After all, for Lucy, this was the journey of a lifetime, a journey of hope. "What a ride!" she thought.

The bus left despite the unusual weather and the fact that neither Lucy nor any of the other passengers had any idea how long the journey might take. Slow and steady went the bus.

Sitting in her office in the South Bronx, Lucy thought, "It's amazing how smooth the ride was at the beginning." She remembered having so much fun on this part of the ride. Her energy level was high and she wondered why some of the passengers were beginning to complain about how rough the ride was becoming.

"I thought we were on the same bus." said Lucy to the passenger sitting next to her. She was shocked when the passenger replied, "Maybe your attitude is what makes the ride easier for you than I".

Just as the bus made a turn, Lucy felt a lump in her

stomach as it hit and unexpected bump. Before she knew it she felt a rush of wind coming through the window next to her. She wondered why the ride had suddenly becomes so uncomfortable. The easy part of the journey had disappeared, although the excitement remained. There were many more bumps and turns to come. Where would she find money to pay for teacher certification, who would hire her, how would she plan units and lessons, where would she find support. "What a ride!" she thought.

But no matter how bumpy, Lucy's dream of a future as a classroom teacher working with students in poor communities, sharing her story, supporting students' learning…and perhaps most important of all…helping instill the belief in her young students that they too had the capacity to achieve anything they strove for, helped her weather the storm and ride out the bumps.

Lucy stood up from behind her desk and looked out of her office window at the sunny day outside. It reminded her of the day, so long ago, that she stepped off the bus that had taken her so far from her home. The weather had cleared, the sun was out and shining. Looking back over the years she realized the ride had been flawless. "I've come so far."

Lucy knew there were many bumps to come, but as she peered out her office window her reflection revealed a smile of gratitude with just a hint of her special gift…belief in herself and her unwavering hope for the future. "What a ride! What an amazing ride!"

The Eternal Yes

There's a dark side to each and every human soul. We wish we were Obi-Wan Kenobi, and for the most part we are, but there's a little Darth Vader in all of us. Thing is, this ain't no either-or proposition. We're talking about dialectics, the good and the bad merging into us. You can run but you can't hide. My experience? Face the darkness. Stare it down. Own it. As brother Nietzsche said, being human is a complicated gig. So give that ol' dark night of the soul a hug. Howl the eternal yes!

> —Monologue by the character Chris Stevens
> on the television show *Northern Exposure*

Old Celtic Blessing

May the blessing of light be on you - light without
    and light within.
May the blessed sunlight shine on you like
    a great peat fire,
so that stranger and friend may come and
    warm himself at it.

And may light shine out of the two eyes of you,
like a candle set in the window of a house,
bidding the wanderer come in out of the storm.

And may the blessing of the rain be on you,
may it beat upon your Spirit and wash it fair and clean,
and leave there a shining pool where
    the blue of Heaven shines,
and sometimes a star.

And may the blessing of the earth be on you,
soft under your feet as you pass along the roads,
soft under you as you lie out on it,
tired at the end of day;
and may it rest easy over you when,
at last, you lie out under it.
May it rest so lightly over you
that your soul may be out from under it quickly
up and on its way to eternity.

Bless the Routine

Bless the remarkable landscape of our gardens:
yellow buses unloading,
students awakening,
drowsily stepping to the curb,
colleagues hurrying into the building,
steam rising from oversized coffee mugs,
bells and announcements,
lockers slamming,
multicolored backpacks overflowing,
hustling through energetic halls
edged with bright bulletin boards,
greetings, casual conversations,
classroom doors closing,
the languid voices of teachers
beginning their lessons,
and always the faces
and presence of children.

The Prophet (Excerpt)
KAHLIL GIBRAN

Our children are not your children.
They are the sons and the daughters of Life's longing for itself.
They come through you but they are not from you,
And though they are with you yet they belong not to you.
You may give them your love but not your thoughts
For they have their own thoughts…
You may strive to be like them, but seek not to make them like you.

The Last Day of School

Ending a school year can be bitter-sweet. We may feel ready to move on but there is often a sadness as we say good-bye to the many students we have come to know, and as we close the door on the emotional blood, sweat, and tears we've poured into our classrooms over the long school year.

And now, on the last day,
at the end of your long journey,
you stop to celebrate what you can
before each of your triumphs and failures
fades into hazy memory and disappears
like the tops of the distant green mountains
gone to the embrace of soft grey clouds.

A voice whispers to you gently,
like a mother calling a child from a day of
    ecstatic play
to an evening routine of chores, dinner, and sleep,

"This is a day to bless, a day to remember.
It can never be repeated, or recreated.
But every day must end."

May you find within that ending its special gift.

This is a day for appreciation

and deep gratitude for the beautiful garden
you have been privileged to tend.
Now is the time to feel the fullness of its harvest,
each of your students grown in body, heart,
    and mind,
no longer the same as on the first day,
and you too, different,
altered by the experience,
traces of the rich earth you worked with care
    each day
still on your hands.

May you be thankful for the path that brought you
    to this place,
and for the colleagues who traveled with you
on a road familiar only to those pilgrims
who walk guided by an inner light called 'teacher'.

This day is a solstice marking the passing of time,
like the pause between breaths.

Put down your burden.
Trust in the seasons,
for when the time is right
you will begin the cycle of learning anew,
for in every ending is born the possibility of
    a new beginning.

Your silent prayer is that you have planted seeds,
that you have nourished your students' gifts,
and that you have set them on the road to learning.

On this last day,
as your paths diverge…

May you all travel safely.

For Your Retirement

PART I - LOOKING BACK

You were given this life to do great things,
and you have.

The years have come and gone,
young faces you've taught
men and women now.

You've traveled a long way
to reach this stony windblown summit,
a wild journey filled with joy and pain,
as is all good work.

It took effort and will to prepare yourself
for this long journey,
and practice to cultivate the elements of mastery
that lay waiting within you.

The courage of your heart
called you to explore the warm upward thermals
that you rode in spiraling circles
to great heights in the crystal blue sky.

From your humble place in the classroom
you have served well,

given birth to new life,
built a grand cathedral of light
shaping and placing each stone with your own hands.

Working with young minds,
curious spirits, and restless hearts was exciting.
Their energy has nourished you
as you have nourished them;
and though they have no way to tell you,
you have left a mark on them,
and through them on the world.
The seeds you have planted
will bloom in times and places
you'll never see.

The great mystery is that by unselfishly giving
    your heart,
whether to the ready and able,
the lost and searching,
or those broken and in pain,
your heart's capacity grew in the giving.

You sacrificed
and through sacrifice learned compassion.
You loved the ones that were hard to love
and through this loving learned to love yourself.

It was by embracing each individual

that you learned to heal, guide, and support;
and it was in the doing and the giving,
that you found your own
healing, guidance, and support.

The measure of your success
is found not only in test scores,
but in the learning that stays with a child
when they've forgotten the dates,
the formulas, and the facts.
Your greatest success has been
living the curriculum of the heart.

PART II - LOOKING FORWARD

Now, as you approach your retirement
remember that all that has gone before
has prepared you for this,
and even on the last day there is something to be learned.
May you be open to that learning.

The spring of a new season is upon you,
time slower and more precious.
You leave the domain of work
with deeper depths of soul to explore.
Face to face with yourself,
with few distractions,
learning to love not only that part of yourself

that 'does',
but finally to indulge and love the stranger that
    simply 'is'.

May you travel many new roads,
and see familiar paths with fresh eyes.

May you find new friends,
while deepening bonds with those
who've loved you these many years.

May you effortlessly make the transition to "elder",
foregoing righteous sermons,
instead selflessly serving others,
not content to relive past glories,
but embracing your hard won wisdom.

May you begin a new resume built on the work
    of the heart.

May your dreams unrealized, be fulfilled.
May you have long health,
light on the darkest nights,
and the courage to live
in the realm of the heart
without fear.

CONTRIBUTORS

JEANNE DENNEY is a therapist, teacher, hospice worker and death (and life) educator who maintains a private practice in Core Energetic Therapy, Somatic Psychology and Energetic Bodywork in Haverstraw, NY and New York City. She is also a poet, bridge engineer, birth doula and has raised four children. Her deepest commitment in life is teaching about patterns within health, transformation and human development derived from a wide lens and deep understanding of the human journey, including birth and death. From there she very much enjoys offering healing, therapy and hospice support in their myriad forms.

www.jeannedenney.com

CHASE MIELKE is a teacher, educational trainer, writer, and speaker from Kalamazoo, Michigan. He has designed and teaches an award winning Positive Psychology program for at-risk sophomores and travels the country to collaborate with teachers and students on how to find more meaning, motivation, and resilience in their lives. Along with his passion for positive psychology, he is a national facilitator for The Quantum Learning Network and a regular contributor to the WeAreTeachers blog. His work and passion for teaching have earned him a 2014 nomination for Michigan Teacher of the Year and an Outstanding People for Education award for Allegany County.

www.affectiveliving.wordpress.com

DENNIS MOORMAN is a Maryknoll Missioner and a Roman Catholic priest. Originally, from rural southeastern Indiana, Dennis holds a Bachelor's degree in Agronomy from Purdue University, a Master's degree in Plant Physiology from North Carolina State University and a Master of Divinity degree from Catholic Theological Union in Chicago. Dennis currently lives in São Paulo, Brazil and devotes his energies to helping heal generational trauma, integrating his expertise in Somatic Experiencing® for the renegotiation of trauma and Family Constellations Systems Therapy. Dennis has worked internationally with helping people heal from trauma in Bolivia, Brazil, Haiti, Hong Kong, Korea and Japan. In this spare time, Dennis enjoys training Aikido, a non-violent, non-competitive Japanese martial art.

dennis.Moorman@gmail.com

DR. PATRICK AWOSOGBA is the founding principal of Mott Hall Science and Technology Academy; an International Baccalaureate authorized middle school located in the South Bronx. Prior to becoming the principal of Mott Hall, Dr. Awosogba served in leadership positions in Bedford Stuyvesant for twelve years as Assistant Principal and a Site Director of an Alternative Learning Center. Dr. Awosogba is a career changer who holds a Master of Business Administration degree (MBA) from St. John's University in Queens, New York.; he is also a graduate of the New Leader's program, a principal leadership preparation program. Dr. Awosogba is an open-minded, enthusiastic leader with a strong commitment to high academic achievement and healthy personal growth of students.

pawosogba@motthallsta.org

CITATIONS

The Journey

Hear the Wind - Marilyn Whirlwind on the television show Northern Exposure, The Blessing Files
https://blessingfiles.wordpress.com

Teacher's Prayer - Author Unknown

A Student of Silence - Jeanne Denney MA, P.E.

The Pointer - Zen Story

What It Means to Teach – (from a story told by Robert Hubsher)

Challenges

The Guest House - *The Essential Rumi* by Jalal al-Din Rumi (Author), Coleman Barks (Translator), HarperOne; Reprint edition; 2004

Holding - Chase Mielke

Helping the Student Who Has Suffered Trauma - Fr. Dennis Moorman

Avoiding Resistance - Fr. Dennis Moorman

Getting Unstuck - Fr. Dennis Moorman

The Smuggler and the Sheriff - Middle Eastern Folktale

Good and Evil - Author Unknown

Insults - Zen Story

A Ute Blessing - Author Unknown, The Blessing Files
https://blessingfiles.wordpress.com

The Heart

Imperfection - Chinese Folk Tale

Surrender - Zen Story

Imperfection - *Kintsugi*, Japanese Decorative Art

Resentment - Two Monks and a Woman - Zen Story

Failure - Excerpts from *The Man Watching*, Rainer Maria
Rilke, From *Selected Poems of Rainer Maria Rilke*, by Robert
Bly. Harper 1981

The Harvest

The Call to Live Everything - Excerpt from *Walking on the
Pastures of Wonder, John O'Donohue in Conversation with John
Quinn*, Veritas 2015

Teachers Wanted: Must Love Students - Keith W. Frome - Letter to the Editor, Buffalo, May 1, 2007

Celtic Prayer - Author Unknown, The Blessing Files
https://blessingfiles.wordpress.com

Where the Answers Live - Irish Folktale told by Johnny Daly, Storyteller, Dublin, Ireland

The Golden Wake - Zen Story

Peace of Mind - Zen Story

Tao Te Ching - Lao Tzu

Hold On - Pueblo Verse, The Blessing Files
https://blessingfiles.wordpress.com

What a Ride! - Dr. Patrick B. Awosogba, Sr.

The Eternal Yes - Chris Stevens on the television show Northern Exposure, The Blessing Files
https://blessingfiles.wordpress.com

Old Celtic Blessing - Author Unknown, The Blessing Files
https://blessingfiles.wordpress.com

The Prophet - Kahil Gibran, Alfred A. Knopf; 1923

ACKNOWLEDGMENTS

It's been a year since I published, *A Path With Heart: The Inner Journey to Teaching Mastery* and since then I've been privileged to share its message with many educators throughout North America. The more I've had a chance to work with the dedicated individuals who commit their lives to educating our young people the more I realize how truly difficult their work is. The classroom I stood in many years ago seems so simple now when compared to the complex environments that they've become. My wife and daughter, both excellent teachers, navigate these waters daily and I see, firsthand, the commitment and sacrifice it takes to fulfill their calling. This book is an acknowledgment of their work and the work of every teacher who knows there is more to teaching than curriculum and pedagogy.

I want to thank Courtney Davis, the Welsh painter, now living in Ireland, who suggested I walk down a quiet lane near his studio in Ireland and look for a little path that would lead me to the Sacred Well of Tara. The world is full of miracles and magic and connecting to Courtney and the Sacred Well was a great blessing. It was my visit to the Well of Tara that inspired me to put aside my plans to write a book on leadership and focus on exploring the beauty of blessings and to follow the voice of my own heart which called me to support the hearts of teachers.

I'd also like to thank the four outstanding 'teachers-educators-leaders' who contributed material for this book: Jeanne Denney, Fr. Dennis Moorman, Chase Mielke, and Dr. Patrick B. Awosogba. Each has amazing and unique gifts which they offer up to the world every day, selflessly. I feel privileged to be able to share their work with you.

Tom McKeveny, my talented, longtime friend, has once again created a wonderfully elegant book design and cover. As part of our work together, Tom and I had to schedule many working lunches, which, no matter how much real work got done, was a wonderful by-product of the publishing process.

I couldn't have written this book without the inspiration of the late John O'Donohue who brought the art of the blessing to its highest form in his magnificent book, *To Bless the Space Between Us*. I bow to him and his unmatched brilliance.

ABOUT THE AUTHOR

Pete Reilly is the author of *A Path with Heart: The Inner Journey to Teaching Mastery*. He is lifelong educator, former English teacher, and educational administrator. Pete has served as coach, mentor, and consultant to many school superintendents, district administrative teams, and classroom teachers. He has devoted his entire professional life to empowering students, teachers, and administrators to fully utilize their unique gifts and talents.

Pete is the former Director of the Lower Hudson Regional Information Center of Southern Westchester BOCES and has served as President of the New York Association of Computers and Technology for Education (NYSCATE). Pete founded the widely acclaimed, Technology Leadership Institute, and has received many educational honors, including being inducted into the NYSCATE Hall of Fame, and being recognized as "Outstanding Administrator" by the Lower Hudson Council of School Administrators.

Pete holds a black belt in Aikido and is a certified Master Somatic Coach. He has designed and delivered many programs that support teachers and administrators in developing the skills they need to be more effective in their work.

ALSO BY PETE REILLY

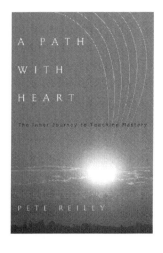

A Path with Heart: *The Inner Journey to Teaching Mastery*

PETE REILLY invites us to approach Teaching Mastery as a hero's journey, one of personal and professional self-discovery. Teachers on the path to Mastery understand that it's not only what they "know" about their subject and pedagogy that determines their effectiveness; but also how well they know their students and themselves.

A Path with Heart blends classroom stories, anecdotes, research, and poetry with concrete practices and activities to assist educators in improving their craft. It's a practical guide for teachers willing to walk a road 'less travelled,' a path of self reflection, self-awareness, and practice.

WEBSITE: www.petereilly.org
E-MAIL: pete@petereilly.org
BLOG: www.petereilly.org/blog
FACEBOOK: www.facebook.com/apathwithheart
TWITTER: www.twitter.com/preilly

PRAISE FOR *A Path With Heart*

This book isn't just about teaching mastery....it shows us the path to life mastery. —JON JANKUS, Managing Director, Guardian Life Insurance

Reilly writes from his own experience as a teacher, but the wisdom and lessons can be applied to any role in every industry. —JEFF CHAPSKI, author of *Career-ology: The Art and Science of a Successful Career*

My son, who is a Junior in High School, wants to be a teacher. I told him before he considers going into the profession he must take the journey with Pete Reilly to determine if he has the heart to be an effective teacher. —PARENT

I completely enjoyed finding my way down "the Path With Heart." I have been teaching for 15 years. I feel as if I have re-found purpose in my chosen career and may be better equipped to face the challenges handed to me every day. —J. SEGALOFF, Middle School Mathematics teacher

This is much more than a book about teaching. Pete Reilly has done an excellent job is showing how being present can not only increase the opportunities you can be for others but also in living a more fulfilled life yourself. —MATT ODELL, Vice President Custom Sales (Global), at Clarity Custom Integration inc.

With over 30 years in education as a teacher and school counselor I feel this book is long over due! It is an easy read that inspires, entertains and is thought provoking. It gives you the gift of tools to use in your classroom to practice, reflect and get into action to make changes to be a better person, teacher. This book needs to be shared with all teachers and administrators to be read and used. We owe this to ourselves and our students. —GRACE

A Path with Heart shows how a teacher, how anyone, can inspire others from within using practical, easily developed "soft skills". Trust, respect, honesty

flowing from teacher to student and back is goal that can be achieved.
—MARK SAMIS, Data Warehouse Manager

This book is not only for teachers but anyone who works with children in an educational setting. It is wonderful how Pete joins teaching, stress management & passion into one book. It actually made me feel more passionate about my interactions with students each day in my role as a School Nurse. I realized how my attitude when I approach students does have an impact on how they will respond to me. I will be sharing the information about this book with my friends who are teachers. Thank you, Pete, for sharing your story and your passion. —PEGGY ECKSTEIN, School Nurse

As a teacher, I was particularly drawn to the classroom stories and anecdotes Pete wrote to illustrate important keys to self-discovery. His suggestions for reflections and actions create a road map for becoming more effective as a teacher. Drawing on his many years of classroom teaching and working with teachers as administrator, instructor, and coach, Pete weaves concrete examples of classroom experiences with his knowledge of personal change to create a guide to improved teaching and learning.
—BONNIE KEAST, Writer, Educator, and Coach

Anyone considering a career in teaching would be well served to read this book. Teaching is not for the faint of heart and Pete calls on all teachers to understand and embrace teaching as a journey of self discovery and not a clinical exercise in the delivery of skilled instruction. Pete understands that teaching well demands that we take risks, that we look inward, that we too embrace change. Pete's book illustrates that one can not truly educate without understanding that establishing and maintaining relationships with our students is fundamental to the teaching process and that there is a pathway, a roadmap for getting there. Pete does not reject data and accountability but he does raise the discussion of teacher quality to the level it deserves.
—GERALD GOLDMAN, Former Superintendent Saranac Lake Central Schools

Pete is not "preaching" a new idea, but sharing his stories of choices taken, lessons learned and rewards received. Pete knows that learning isn't just about the mind. Pete writes in the mold of Parker Palmer extolling us to be the greatest teacher we can be because the life of our students depends on it. I loved this book and recommend it highly.

—THOMAS WHITE, CEO, C-Suite Network

Our Power to Bless One Another
John O'Donohue

In the parched deserts of postmodernity a blessing can be like
the discovery of a fresh well. It would be lovely if we could
rediscover our power to bless one another. I believe each
of us can bless. When a blessing is invoked, it changes the
atmosphere. Some of the plenitude flows into our hearts from
the invisible neighborhood of loving kindness. In the light and
reverence of blessing, a person or situation becomes illuminated
in a completely new way. In a dead wall a new window opens,
in dense darkness a path starts to glimmer, and into a broken
heart healing falls like morning dew. It is ironic that so often
we continue to live like paupers though our inheritance of spirit
is so vast. The quiet eternal that dwells in our souls is silent
and subtle; in the activity of blessing it emerges to embrace
and nurture us. Let us begin to learn how to bless one another.
Whenever you give a blessing, a blessing returns to enfold you.

Excerpt from *To Bless the Space Between Us*

ABOUT THE TYPE

This book is set in Caslon. The original font, first cut by Willam Caslon in 1725, was widely used, including for the Declaration of Independence. This version, created for Adobe Systems typography division by Carol Twombly and issued in 1990, makes an elegant and classic impression.

The font used for headings, set larger than the text, is Spectrum, introduced by Monotype Image Holdings in 1955. Though rooted in the great Aldine types of Venice, the letterforms have a crisp, contemporary feel.